Summer Style

Summer Style

Decorating Ideas & Projects
for Outdoor Living

paige gilchrist

LARK BOOKS

A DIVISION OF
STERLING PUBLISHING CO., INC.
NEW YORK, NY

EDITOR:
PAIGE GILCHRIST

ART DIRECTOR:
CHRIS BRYANT

PHOTOGRAPHY:
WRIGHT CREATIVE
PHOTOGRAPHY & DESIGN

PHOTO STYLIST:
SKIP WADE

COVER DESIGN:
BARBARA ZARETSKY

ILLUSTRATOR:
BERNADETTE WOLF
(WITH ILLUSTRATIONS ON PAGES 41
AND 125 BY CHRIS BRYANT)

ASSISTANT EDITOR:
RAIN NEWCOMB

PRODUCTION ASSISTANTS:
HANNES CHAREN
SHANNON YOKELEY

EDITORIAL ASSISTANTS:
DELORES GOSNELL
VERONIKA ALICE GUNTER
HEATHER SMITH

INTERNS:
LORELEI BUCKLEY, ART
HELENA KNOX, EDITORIAL
BRIAN SMITH, EDITORIAL

SPECIAL PHOTOGRAPHY:
EVAN BRACKEN

SANOMA SYNDICATION:
Dennis Brandsma

Library of Congress Cataloging-in-Publication Data

Gilchrist, Paige.
   Summer style : decorating ideas and projects for
outdoor living / by Paige Gilchrist.—1st ed.
      p. cm.
   Includes index.
   ISBN 1-57990-344-4 (hard)
   1. Handicraft. 2. Outdoor living spaces—
Decoration. 3. House furnishings I. Title.
   TT157.G4573 2003
   745'.5—dc21   2002034393

10 9 8 7 6 5 4 3 2 1
First Edition

Published by Lark Books,
a division of Sterling Publishing Co., Inc.
387 Park Avenue South, New York, N.Y. 10016

© 2003, Lark Books

Distributed in Canada by Sterling Publishing,
c/o Canadian Manda Group, One Atlantic Ave., Suite 105
Toronto, Ontario, Canada M6K 3E7

Distributed in the U.K. by Guild of Master Craftsman Publications Ltd.,
Castle Place, 166 High Street, Lewes, East Sussex, England BN7 1XU
Tel: (+ 44) 1273 477374, Fax: (+ 44) 1273 478606
Email: pubs@thegmcgroup.com, Web: www.gmcpublications.com

Distributed in Australia by Capricorn Link (Australia) Pty Ltd.,
P.O. Box 704, Windsor, NSW 2756 Australia

The written instructions, photographs, designs, patterns, and projects in this volume are intended for the personal use of the reader and may be reproduced for that purpose only. Any other use, especially commercial use, is forbidden under law without written permission of the copyright holder.

Every effort has been made to ensure that all the information in this book is accurate. However, due to differing conditions, tools, and individual skills, the publisher cannot be responsible for any injuries, losses, and other damages that may result from the use of the information in this book.

If you have questions or comments about this book, please contact:
Lark Books • 67 Broadway, Asheville, NC 28801 • (828) 236-9730

acknowledgments

Much thanks to the generous folks who welcomed our cameras and crew into their stylish summer locations:

- The residents of **Breezemont Cottage** in the historic Albamarle Park neighborhood of Asheville, North Carolina

- **Mark** and **Vicki Maurer**
  Wright Inn & Carriage House
  www.wrightinn.com

- **Allison Smith** and **Bill "Tama" Dickerson**
  Water Rock Garden Retreat
  www.waterrockgarden.com

- **Heather Spencer** and **Charles Murray**

And special thanks to Assistant Editor **Rain Newcomb**, who got into the summer spirit when temperatures were still well below freezing. Her savvy research and smart writing are evident throughout the book's sidebars.

contents

Introduction, 8

78 gathering

102 lounging in the shade

summer style

> *"Summer afternoon...*
> *to me those have always been*
> *the two most beautiful words*
> *in the English language."*
> — Henry James

MY FIRST GUESS WAS THAT JAMES CAME TO THIS CON-
CLUSION IN THE MIDDLE OF A JANUARY BLIZZARD.
The room was dark, his hands were chapped, he was
wearing two layers of long underwear, and the first fresh
vegetables were still six months away. But actually, no.
He tossed off the observation while sprawled on the
lawn with friends, relishing the real thing.

Of course. Summer is one of those rare pleasures in
life that's somehow even better in reality than it is in
our imaginations. Maybe that's because its joys are so
enchantingly simple—going barefoot, jumping off the
dock, eating an ice cream cone, staying up late—that
fantasies have a hard time competing. This book of
summertime decorating ideas and projects is dedicated
to the spirit of those simple joys.

Summer is when porches, decks, patios, and yards
become our prime living and entertaining spots, giving
us a whole new focus for all sorts of seasonal touches.
It's also when we have an irrepressible urge to invite
people over and celebrate—the warming temperatures,
the long days, the growing gardens, and the fact that
we can't help but feel we're on a bit of a vacation, even
if we are just sitting in the yard sipping iced tea. The
trouble is that we're as interested in labor-intensive
decorating projects this time of year as we are in
putting on a heavy coat and scraping ice off the wind-
shield. This book is full of dozens of ways to dress up
your outdoor spaces, keeping in mind all the while
that the living really is supposed to be easy.

introduction

Summer Romance

The book's first chapter features ideas and projects for celebrating your love affair with the season, from filmy throw pillows for outdoor furniture, to candles, canopies, and a setting for a French country picnic.

Summers Past

If spring is a time of rebirth, we spend the summer immersed in the carefree abandon of youth. Like some help recapturing it? There are projects for a decorated swing, garlands of daisy chains, red wagons transformed into party seating, and more. We also give you ideas for reliving the good old days (whether you actually experienced them or just wish you had), such as a table setting featuring vintage collections of plates and glassware and a plan for reviving an antique lawn chair.

In Bloom

This chapter showcases summer's blossoms and other bounty. We show you how to turn lush images from garden catalogs into coasters for cold drinks, use sprigs of ferns and ivy to stamp an elegant set of table linens, combine pressed flowers and a candle to create a radiant centerpiece, plus give you other ideas for playing up what's prettiest about summer.

Gathering

You need table coverings for cookouts, lighting for nighttime parties, holders for candles, vases for flowers, food covers, centerpieces, and more. We cover it all, with everything from an easier-than-batik polka-dot tablecloth to a brilliant bouquet of glowsticks.

Lounging in the Shade

Aristotle said that happiness depends on leisure. This chapter is designed to make you ecstatic—not to mention cool—with projects such as cocktail parasols, handmade fans, a deck awning, and a painted lemonade pitcher. We even include tips on buying and hanging a hammock.

Scattered throughout are tributes to summer's irresistible rituals, customs, and lore. You can use them to sharpen your stargazing skills, review the basics of assembling s'mores, learn how to blend a perfect watermelon smoothie, and remind yourself of the long and happy tradition of the summer siesta.

If you're paging through this book in the midst of your own blissful summer afternoon, pick a project and plunge in. Most are so breezy and easy, you'll whip them up for a single occasion. A few others—the porch swing cover, maybe, or the giant floral throw cushions—you'll probably want to make early in the season, then show off all summer long.

If it's January and snowing, keep reading, and hang in there.

Summer Romance

Shall I compare thee to a summer's day?
— William Shakespeare

1

SUMMER STYLE

starlit plates

Some hazy summer evenings, it's impossible to coax the heavens into providing the twinkling canopy you had in mind for an intimate outdoor meal. Use this easy technique to etch your own plates (not to mention platters, bowls, and glasses), and you can still guarantee a starry night.

DESIGNER: **ALLISON SMITH**

WHAT YOU NEED

Newspaper
Plain glass plates
Large, repositionable star stickers
Etching cream (sold by the bottle at craft stores)
Rubber gloves
Small paintbrush
Plain glass plates

WHAT YOU DO

1 Cover your work surface with several layers of newspaper.

2 Position star stickers on the back side of a plate.

3 Wearing rubber gloves, use the paintbrush to cover the back of the plate with a heavy coat of etching cream. Allow the cream to process according to package instructions.

4 Wash the plate thoroughly with warm water.

5 Remove the stickers and wash the plate again with soap and warm water. Repeat the process to etch your other plates.

WHAT YOU NEED

9 yards (8.1 m) of plain white canvas,
    42 inches (106.7 cm) wide

Scissors

Sewing machine

Heavy-weight thread in a
    polyester-cotton blend

Straight pins

⅝-inch (1.6 cm) grommets

4 8-foot (240 cm) wooden poles

Handsaw

Drill and drill bit

Sandpaper

4 ¼-inch (6 mm) double-ended screws

4 feet (120 cm) of 1-x-1 pine board

Cotton rope

DESIGNER: **ALLISON SMITH**

picnic canopy

*This airy canvas canopy transforms your favorite backyard picnic spot into an
intimate oasis, perfect for all sorts of summer retreating. Use it to set the stage
for everything from coffee and the morning paper to candlelit dinners.*

WHAT YOU DO

1 Cut two 3-yard (2.7 m) panels of canvas. An easy way to do this is to simply snip the edge of the canvas and tear it to length.

2 Create one large panel by sewing the two canvas panels together lengthwise, wrong sides facing, then use a French seam to hide the raw edges. To sew a French seam, trim the seam allowances and press them open. Fold the fabric at the seam, right sides facing (the raw edge will be hidden), and press again. Sew along the inside edge with a ⅝-inch (1.6 cm) seam allowance. Unfold the fabric and press again on the seam.

3 Tear or cut the remaining 3 yards (2.7 m) of fabric lengthwise into four strips, each 10 inches (25.4 cm) wide. On two of the strips, using a ⅝-inch (1.6 cm) seam allowance, hem both short ends and one long edge.

4 Measure the width of the large fabric panel. Add 1½ inches (3.8 cm) for a seam allowance, then cut the two unhemmed strips to this length. Hem the ends and the raw edges on the long sides of these strips.

5 Pin the strips to the main canopy. Attach them with a French seam, as described in step 2.

6 Attach a grommet at each corner, following the instructions on the grommet packaging.

7 Use a handsaw to cut off 12 inches (30.5 cm) from the ends of two of the wooden poles. Cut four 3-inch (7.6 cm) pieces from the scrap to make finials.

8 Drill ¼-inch (6 mm) holes into one end of each canopy pole and into one end of each finial. Smooth the rough edges with sandpaper. Screw one end of a double-ended screw into each of the canopy poles.

9 Cut the pine board into four 12-inch (30.5 cm) pieces to create stakes. Sand the ends, and drill a hole through each stake about 2 inches (5.1 cm) down from the top.

10 Cut four 15-inch (38.1 cm) lengths of cotton rope. Tie a small loop on the end of each rope.

11 Attach the poles to the canopy by threading the screws through the corner grommets, then adding the finials. Attach the 8-inch (20.3 cm) poles on one side and the 7-inch (17.8 cm) poles on the other.

12 Stand the canopy up on the poles. You might need an extra person to keep it balanced while you secure the tent stakes. Drive the tent stakes into the ground about 4 feet (120 cm) from the tent poles on all four corners. Loop one end of the cotton rope around a corner finial. Thread the other end through the hole in the tent stake. Pull tightly, wrap the rope around the stake a few times, and tie it. Repeat on the other three corners.

french country picnic setting

One of the most alluring aspects of summertime is its aura of indulgence and escape. To give yourself over to it completely, put away the plastic plates, and spread out a setting of casual luxury.

DESIGNER: **KENNETH TRUMBAUER**

The enduring appeal of French country style is that it's elegant and, at the same time, gracious and inviting. That combination also makes it easy to achieve. Simply transport some standard indoor items, from colored-glass platters to oversize throw pillows, to your outdoor setting, where they'll take on a whole new life. The key is to not get overly fussy with accessories and accents, but to choose a few key embellishments and play them up.

COLOR

Unify your setting by choosing two or three colors to showcase. We started with a navy tablecloth, then crisscrossed it with two sunny marigold runners. Toss this crisp, classic combination on the ground rather than over a dining table, and it captures the irresistible Provençal blend of refined and rustic. The rest of the setting's elements echo this color combination, with wisps of white added here and there to soften it.

GLASS & CHINA

One of the simplest ways to make an outdoor setting special is to add the sparkle of real glass and china. We incorporated both clear glass goblets and cobalt blue serving pieces, and let salad plates serve as coasters. If you have them, add silver pieces, such as serving spoons and cake knives, to the setting. Family heirlooms that show years of use help emphasize the traditional mood.

COMFORT

How do you keep a polished outdoor setting from feeling too prim and proper? Make sure it's obvious to all that lounging and luxuriating are a definite part of the plan. Here, we communicate that concept by surrounding the setting with large body pillows wrapped in navy covers that match the cloth.

FLOWERS

Another way to keep a special setting from feeling too formal is to fill a crystal vase with flowers that look as if they were picked from a nearby sun-drenched field rather than chosen from a refrigerated florist's case. We used a cheerful mix of blue delphinium, delicate Queen Anne's lace, and big, friendly sunflowers, all in keeping with the color scheme.

VARIETY

The less static your setting, the more inviting. We added movement to this one by incorporating pieces of varying heights, from the tiered baker's stand, which acts as a serving tray, to the mosaic vase doing duty as a wine bucket.

"**A** JUG OF WINE, A LOAF OF BREAD, AND THOU**" is right. One of the great undisputed truths of summer is that if you spread a blanket down outside and cover it with food and drink, the most ordinary of meals becomes a celebratory feast.

PICNIC PREPAREDNESS

basic checklist

- ☑ Tablecloth
- ☑ Plates
- ☑ Cups or glasses
- ☑ Utensils
- ☑ Napkins
- ☐ Towelettes
- ☐ Cutting board
- ☑ Corkscrew
- ☑ Salt & pepper
- ☑ Insect repellant
- ☐ Citronella candles & matches
- ☑ Sunscreen
- ☑ Trash bags
- ☐ Flashlight

highly subjective list of other essentials

- ☑ Guitar or other musical instruments
- ☑ Book of poems
- ☐ Frisbee, beach ball, or baseball and mitt
- ☑ Vase for fresh flowers you can pick at your site
- ☑ Camera
- ☐ Journal
- ☑ Pillow for napping
- ☐ The dog

PACKING YOUR HAMPER

■ If you're going farther than the backyard, consider how travel-friendly a food is before you add it to your menu. Foods that don't slosh around and require only hands or one utensil to eat are usually better than elaborate dishes that require lots of serving and eating fuss.

■ It's typically easier to keep cold foods cold than hot foods piping hot, so steer away from anything that will suffer if it's lukewarm instead of steaming.

■ Pack last what you'll need first, and you won't have to dig around looking for the picnic blanket underneath the dessert. The exception to this rule is raw meat in a cooler full of other perishables. Always pack it on the bottom, to keep it from dripping onto other foods.

■ Cut meats, cakes, and casseroles before leaving home, then wrap them tightly so they don't dry out.

■ Stack flat foods (cookies, sandwiches, etc.) in plastic containers, with wax paper between each layer.

■ Pack frozen gel packs in the cooler; they last longer than ice and don't make foods soggy. Store the cooler in the shade with a blanket over it for greater insulation, and keep the lid closed as much as possible.

Picnicking

SPUR-OF-THE-MOMENT PICNICKING

Summer is supposed to be about spontaneous fun, which means you may not have time to fry chicken and bake a chocolate pie every time the picnic urge hits. Pick and choose from this list of gourmet-to-go items instead, and you can have your picnic on the road in no time.

- Olives
- Pate
- Tapenade (a spread made of finely chopped olives and capers) or some other packaged spread or dip
- Smoked fish
- Cured salami or sausage

- Focaccia bread and olive oil
- Wedge of cheese
- Fresh fruit
- A dozen cookies from your favorite bakery
- Wine, beer, or imported lemonades, spritzers, ciders, and sparkling sodas

10 ROMANTIC PLACES TO PICNIC

1 Drive-in movie theatre

2 Rowboat on a lake

3 County fairgrounds

4 Outdoor concert or play

5 Winery or vineyard

6 Balcony of a bed & breakfast

7 Tree house

8 City park on your lunch break

9 Botanical garden

10 Orchard

DESIGNER: **ALLISON SMITH**

abalone shell votives

Pearly abalone shell buttons and pastel votives make sweet little lights just right for a pared-down summer setting. They're also so simple to make, you can assemble enough to line a porch railing, a table runner, or the steps to the deck.

WHAT YOU NEED

Waxed linen string in a variety of colors
Small abalone shell buttons
Small straight-sided glass votive holders
Scissors
Colored votive candles

WHAT YOU DO

1 Thread one end of a length of linen string through an abalone shell button, leaving about 3 inches (7.6 cm) of string at the end for tying.

2 Wrap the waxed linen string around the votive holder, then thread it back through the button holes a second time.

3 Pulling the string taunt, wrap the votive holder two more times.

4 Tie the string tightly behind the button. Cut and tuck the ends of the string.

5 Insert a candle in the holder. Repeat the process to create as many candles as you need.

exotica lanterns

You'll find plain paper lanterns for sale everywhere come summertime, ready to add a wispy glow to outdoor gatherings. But if you want yours to cast a more distinctive light—perhaps something like the rich, Indian-motif variations here—all you need are printed paper napkins and decoupage medium.

DESIGNER: **TERRY TAYLOR**

WHAT YOU NEED

Paper lantern
Printed napkins
Sharp scissors
Acrylic decoupage
    medium
Paintbrush
Stencil brush

WHAT YOU DO

1 If your lantern is packaged flat and unassembled (this is typically the case), expand it and insert the wire handle, which prevents it from collapsing.

2 Use sharp scissors to cut out design elements from the napkins. Peel away the white layer of napkin, and set the pieces aside. It's a good idea to cut out more than you think you'll need.

3 Spread a thin coat of decoupage medium on the lantern, covering an area about the size of one of the pieces you cut out. Position a piece on top of the medium.

4 Use the stencil brush to pounce the piece onto the surface of the lantern, then brush the piece with a light coat of decoupage medium.

5 Cover the lantern with the pieces. Let them dry.

6 Give the lantern a final light coat of decoupage medium.

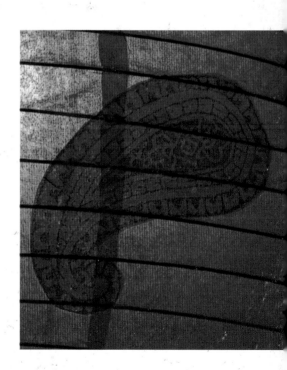

paradise found

You're dreaming of a remote island, but you're landlocked in your own backyard. The answer? Turn a tiny patch of it into a luminous, white-on-white sanctuary, and you have an exotic destination right outside your door. Unlit, it's a shaded getaway during the day. At night, it's a fanciful seating area at a gathering.

WHAT YOU NEED

Large canvas beach umbrella or picnic table umbrella

Strings of white indoor/outdoor lights that can be plugged in end to end

Extension cord(s)

Several yards (m) of white gauze or mosquito netting (Use one huge piece or a number of narrower strips.)

WHAT YOU DO

1 Decide where you want the umbrella, and position it on its side.

2 Run the extension cord from the power source to the umbrella. Now is the time to make sure you have enough cords to reach the umbrella and that you can run them in a way that isn't obtrusive.

3 Plug your first string of lights into the extension cord, wind it around the umbrella's pole, and begin wrapping it around the frame of the umbrella.

4 Wrap the entire frame with lights, plugging in additional strings as you go.

5 Swath the umbrella in gauze or mosquito netting, leaving a tent-like opening for crawling under the umbrella. Add pillows or cushions, if you like.

When you want a break from all the bold, blazing-hot hues of summer, this study in serenity will cool you off and calm you down. It's also a perfect way to show off a small number of single blooms.

bottled flowers

DESIGNER: **KENNETH TRUMBAYER**

WHAT YOU NEED

A collection of bottles in various sizes and shapes (Try antique medicine bottles, your grand-mother's old perfume bottles, and other small vessels. Choose some that are clear and others that are iridescent blue and green.)

Antique mirrored tray (You could also use a silver tray or even white wicker.)

Glass cleaner and rag

Single stems of flowers (We used mini calla lilies. You could also try white or pink roses, pale pansies, or delicate cosmos.)

Scissors

WHAT YOU DO

1 Clean the tray and bottles.

2 Fill the bottles with water and arrange them on the tray. An odd number of bottles works best. Try putting the taller ones in the center first, then position the shorter ones around them.

3 Clean the stems of the flowers, and cut them on an angle, so the flower heights work well with the bottle sizes.

4 Place the flowers in the bottles. If you like, you can leave some bottles empty to add a bit more interest to the display.

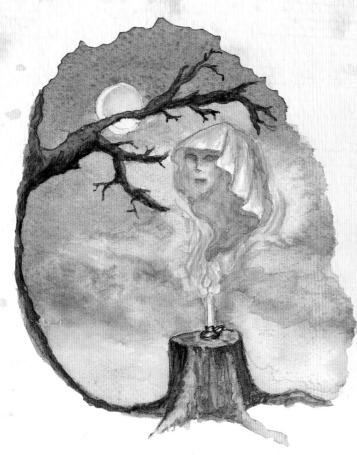

1 Set the mood ahead of time, dropping intriguing little hints about a story you want to tell everyone later—if they're up to it.

2 Lighting is critical. Let the fire die to a low glow. If you don't have a fire, light just a few candles. In a pinch, you can use a flashlight covered with a cloth to soften its beam of light.

3 Tailor your story, making it local and more up-to-date, if you can. The most effective ghost stories are about regular people and set in the recent past.

4 Make the story personal: "My friend has a cousin who was camping once…." or "Just up the road not far from here…"Good ghost stories are usually told as if they're true.

5 Props can help personalize a story—the handkerchief she left behind when she disappeared, or a photograph of the footsteps leading into the woods.

6 Make good use of the dramatic pause. Let the sounds of the night around you creep in. Wait for your audience to urge you to go on.

7 If you think you can pull it off, stop completely before you reach the story's climax to ask if anyone else heard anything ("oh, it was probably nothing"), then search the area with a flashlight to be sure. An out-of-sight accomplice can add effects as subtle as rustling branches or as conspicuous as a blood-curdling scream.

8 Make your finish more riveting by threatening to withhold the ending (you've decided it's just too scary), or by suggesting that you wait to tell how it turns out another time. Your audience will beg you to finish the tale.

THE STARS ARE OUT, THE FIRE IS CRACKLING, COUPLES ARE CUDDLING, AND ALL EYES ARE ON YOU. Waiting. Fortunately, the audience is on your side; most of us love the cathartic rush of a good scare. Follow these basic guidelines, and you'll keep your listeners on the edges of their seats and up all night.

Telling campfire ghost tales

porch swing slipcover

DESIGNER: **TRACY MUNN**

We have no idea exactly how many first kisses occur during moonlit spells on porch swings, but we're betting the number is high. Just think how the statistics would soar if more swings featured cozy, cushioned covers like this one.

summer style

WHAT YOU NEED

About 2½ yards (2.25 m) of fabric for a standard-size swing; this design uses mattress ticking

Piece of polyester batting the size of the swing's seat

Scissors

Standard measuring tools

Straight pins

Long, ready-made upholstery zipper

Chalk marker

Iron

Serger (optional)

Bodkin

Dowel

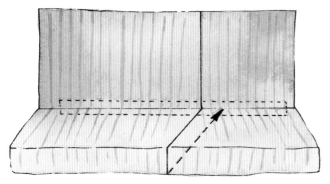

FIGURE 1. Pinned-together cover sections with zipper added. The fabric is folded to define the seat's bottom flap, just below the seat edge.

WHAT YOU DO

1 Cut one piece of fabric that will cover both the swing's inside back and the top and bottom of the seat. It should extend over the front edge of the seat by about 2½ inches (6.4 cm) and continue on to completely cover the bottom side of the seat. Make sure the piece you cut includes seam allowances of 2 inches (5 cm) as well.

2 Cut another piece of fabric for the back of the inside back. In step 5, you'll insert a zipper in the seam where the seat bottom meets the underside of the inside back.

3 To make a flap for the swing's back, cut one piece that matches the measurements of the swing back, plus 2 inches (5 cm) for a hem and 2 inches (5 cm) for seam allowances. You'll also need four ties for this piece, so cut four pieces of fabric, measuring 9 x 3 inches each (22.9 x 7.6 cm).

4 Pin together one long edge of the main section (the piece you cut in step 1) to the piece that will be the back of the inside back, pinning where the back meets the seat.

5 Insert the zipper in the pinned-together seam.

6 Place the fabric on the swing, positioning the zipper where the seat meets the inside back of the swing (see figure 1). Make a fold in the fabric where the bottom of the flap should be on the front of the swing, about 2½ inches (6.4 cm) below the seat edge (again, see figure 1). Pin to hold this fold in place for now. Smooth the fabric along the seat and up the inside back.

7 With a chalk marker on the wrong side of the fabric, mark the exact sides of the swing, where the side seams should be. If you like, taper the inside seams at the inside back, to tailor the cover's fit. Remove the cover, and press the front flap fold. Remove the pins holding the front flap in place.

8 Finish three sides (two short and one long) of the back flap piece by serging and topstitching.

9 Matching centers, pin the back flap to the top edge of the inside back piece, right sides together (see figure 2). Stitch with a basting stitch.

10 Lay the cover out on a large surface (a worktable or the floor), right sides together. Match the side edges of the main piece, so you can sew them. As you do, make sure the folded edge of the front flap is folded back on the pressed fold line. Pin the sides, then stitch along the chalk lines you marked in step 7. Also, stitch the top edge you basted in step 9. Serge all the raw edges. If you don't have a serger, finish the raw edges by overcasting your seams with a zigzag stitch on your sewing machine, or clip them with pinking shears.

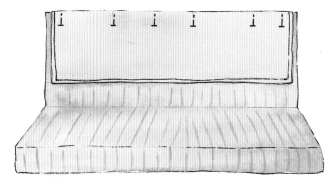

FIGURE 2. Match centers, and pin the back flap to the inside back.

PHOTO 1. Add ties for the back flap.

11 Turn the cover right side out, and topstitch along the front flap fold line you pressed in step 7.

12 Using the four strips you cut in step 3, make four ties for the back flap. Fold each in half lengthwise, right sides together, and stitch, using a standard stitch. Stitch across one end, make a right-angle turn, and continue stitching down the tie's long side, always backstitching at the start and finish. Insert a bodkin, and turn the tie right side out. Use the pointed end of a dowel to push out the corners neatly, and press the tie with an iron. Stitch two of them to the back flap's finished long edge, right at the sides. Stitch the remaining two ties to the bottom of the seat, right at the zipper, making sure they align with the other two ties of the back flap (see photo 1).

13 Cut a piece of polyester batting the exact size of the seat, insert it in the seat area (see photo 2), and zip up the zipper. Put the cover on the swing, tie the ties at the back of the swing, add decorative pillows, and sit down and swing a while.

PHOTO 2. Insert batting in the seat area.

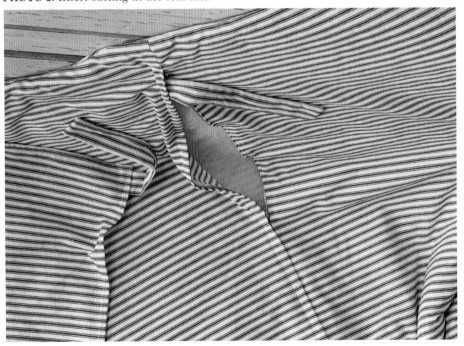

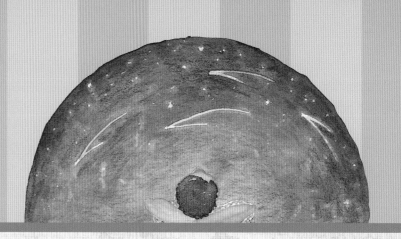

Stargazing

CLEAR NIGHT, WARM BREEZE, AND A BLANKET ON THE GRASS...
the next best thing to gazing into your beloved's eyes is lying back and
looking up. Times when the moon is new or in its waxing or waning phase
are best for viewing the passion play of constellations overhead. Here are some
helpful hints for spotting all the dippers, dragons, deities, and others.

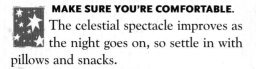

GET AS FAR AWAY FROM CITY LIGHTS AS POSSIBLE. The ideal location for stargazing is an open or a high point with a view of the horizon.

START ABOUT DUSK. Two to three hours after sunset is when the action gets underway, often beginning with satellites you'll see as dots of light moving across the sky. When you finally spot the first star, make a wish, of course.

MAKE SURE YOU'RE COMFORTABLE. The celestial spectacle improves as the night goes on, so settle in with pillows and snacks.

GET A GOOD STAR CHART TO HELP YOU IDENTIFY WHAT'S WHAT. You'll also want a flashlight for checking it. Cover the end of the flashlight with a bandanna or cloth napkin, so its brightness will interfere as little as possible. Binoculars aren't mandatory, but if you've got some, you'll be able to make out more specific stars and planets.

GET YOUR BEARINGS. Your star chart will use some sort of coordinate system for helping you locate stars, planets, and other astronomical objects in the night sky, based on where you are. Typically, it'll refer you to a position on the horizon, then tell you how high above it (usually in the form of degrees) to look. One of the most convenient tools to use in measuring up is your own hand. In general, the width of one finger held out at arm's length is about one degree. A fist is about 10 degrees.

TAKE IT EASY. In case you need reminding, this is summer fun, not an assignment. Don't feel you have to check off all the constellations in one night; it took hundreds of centuries for human beings to identify all the star formations we look for today and to come up with their names and stories.

USE YOUR IMAGINATION. Those names and stories vary from culture to culture and from time period to time period, by the way. If you see a wand instead of a dipper or if the Southern Cross looks more like a computer icon to you, why not create your own modern legend to go with it?

PLANET TRACKING

Planets are easy to distinguish from stars; they're typically brighter, and they don't twinkle.

 Venus is recognizable by its red color.

Jupiter, the largest planet in our solar system, appears cream colored and is second only to Venus in brightness.

Mars, like Venus, is a red planet, but you can tell the two apart because Mars isn't as bright.

Uranus and Neptune, the third- and fourth-largest planets, are so far away you need binoculars for Uranus and a telescope for Neptune.

three dreamy throw pillows

DESIGNER: **DIANA LIGHT**

Toss this dainty trio onto the nearest wicker settee or chaise longue, and wait for it to sweep you off your feet. Once you're settled in with a book of poems (palm-frond fan optional), these pillows will gently lull you into whiling away the dreamiest of summer afternoons.

WHAT YOU NEED

Scissors

Tape measure

Straight edge

Straight pins

Iron

Sewing machine equipped with
    a ballpoint needle suitable for
    lightweight knits, size 80/11

White polyester thread

2 yds (1.8 m) muslin

Polyester stuffing

for pillow #1

⅜ yd (.3 m) white linen cloth

Pencil

2 shades of green embroidery floss

Embroidery needle

Silk flowers

for pillow #2

½ yd (.45 m) pink satin or polyester

½ yd (.45 m) rosebud-embroidered
    white silk

for pillow #3

¾ yd (.67 m) green satin or polyester

¼ yd (.22 m) white silk organza

Green thread to match satin

Silk flowers and leaves

Green embroidery floss

Embroidery needle

WHAT YOU DO

pillow #1 prep

1 Cut two large squares out of the linen.

2 Measure and lightly mark a 10-inch (25.4 cm) square in the center of one linen square. Mark the smaller square with pins.

3 Within the marked square, use the pencil and straight edge to lightly pencil in flowers, stems, and leaves. Make the bottoms of the stems even. Vary their heights and leaf placements.

4 Using four strands of embroidery floss and the embroidery needle, backstitch the stems with darker green and the leaves with lighter green.

5 Stitch a silk flower in place at the top of each stem with an "X" of dark green in the center of each flower.

6 Remove the straight pins.

pillow #2 prep

1 Cut two large squares out of the satin or polyester.

2 Cut a square of embroidered silk the same size as your satin or polyester squares.

3 Pin the silk, face up, to one square of the satin or polyester. Use plenty of pins.

4 Stitch around the pinned pieces with a ⅛-inch (3 mm) seam. Remove the pins.

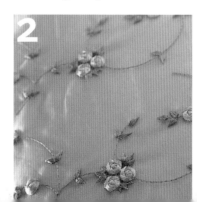

pillow #3 prep

1 Cut two large squares out of the satin or polyester.

2 Cut three squares out of the silk organza, one 5 inches (12.7 cm) square, one 6½ inches (16.5 cm), and one 7½ inches (19.1 cm).

3 Iron each square, then turn under a ⅛-inch (3 mm) hem on all sides of each, and iron the hems down.

4 Arrange and pin one edge of each pocket to the shiny side of one piece of green satin or polyester.

5 Arrange silk flowers and leaves underneath the organza squares, and attach each with a green embroidery-floss "X."

6 Pin the other pocket edges, and stitch all four sides down, using a machine stitch. Stitch around a second time, so you have a double row of stitches, both for a decorative touch and to keep the hems from ravelling.

finishing all pillows

1 Using plenty of pins (about 1 per inch [2.5 cm]), pin the front and back pillow squares together, right sides together. (Pillow #3 is an exception. Pin it with the pocket side facing the wrong side of the satin or polyester, to create a contrast between the front and back of that pillow.)

2 With white thread, stitch ¼ inch (6 mm) in from the edges around each pillow, leaving an opening one-half the length of one side on one side of each pillow.

3 Turn the pillows right side out.

making pillow inserts and stuffing pillows

1 For each pillow, cut two muslin squares the size of the squares you cut for the pillow cover.

2 Sew the muslin squares together with a ¼-inch (6 mm) seam, leaving an opening one-half the length of one side on one side of each pillow.

3 Turn the inserts right side out, and stuff each with filling.

4 Close the inserts by holding the openings closed, with the hems in, and running the openings through the machine, ⅛ to ¼ inch (3 to 6 mm) from the edge.

5 On all three pillow covers, machine stitch a ⅛-inch (3 mm) seam all around the pillows, leaving the openings open. Use white thread on Pillows #1 and #2 and green thread on Pillow #3.

6 Stuff the inserts into the pillows. Close the openings by folding the hems in, pinning them in place, and machine stitching the openings closed, using a ⅛-inch (3 mm) seam.

THE MAGIC OF THE SEASON MAY BE PARTLY RESPONSIBLE FOR THE SEEMINGLY ENDLESS SUMMER DAY. But the long, light hours are thanks primarily to the tinkering most of us do with our clocks each spring, when we leap forward an hour to *daylight saving time*.

The fringed benefit of the annual time change is that we all have more natural-light hours each day for sailing around the sound or strolling through the garden. The original purpose, however, was to conserve energy. Benjamin Franklin proposed the idea of what has become daylight saving time in 1784, during a stay in Paris. In an essay called "An Economical Project," Franklin calculated that Parisians would save 64,050,000 pounds of candle wax and tallow a year simply by waking up before noon. (The city evidently got a late start in those days; even most bakeries were closed in the morning.) Franklin's tongue-in-cheek proposal didn't receive much serious consideration, though. That could have had something to do with the fact that it included suggestions such as setting off canons at daybreak to rouse the sleeping populace.

More than 100 years after Franklin's essay, the idea of saving daylight was reintroduced by a London builder named William Willet. He advocated changing the clocks to take advantage of daylight hours, thereby saving fuel used to light and heat homes. But it wasn't until 1916, a year after Willet's death, that daylight saving time was introduced in several countries in Northern Europe. Today, approximately 70 countries observe the change to what many of them call "summer time."

a light matter

Summers Past

The summer that I was ten—
Can it be there was only one
summer that I was ten?
It must have been
a long one then—

—May Swenson

2
SUMMER STYLE

simple painted swing

DESIGNER: **DIANA LIGHT**

Remember when any trouble in the whole world seemed better if you gave it some thought while pumping your legs and flying back and forth into the sky? Here's an easy way to treat yourself to some back-to-basics problem-solving— and to add a dash of whimsy to the nearest sturdy limb.

WHAT YOU NEED

White pine board, 1 x 8 x 22 inches
  (2.5 x 20.3 x 55.9 cm) (For an extra-strong
  swing, use a 2-inch [5.1 cm] board.)

Sandpaper

Ruler

Pencil

Power drill with a 9/16-inch (1.4 cm)
  wood-boring bit

Latex primer

Flat nylon/polyester brush,
  2 inches (5.1 cm)

Acrylic paints in dark green, green, white,
  yellow, and gold

Sea sponge

Wax paper

Simple Painted Swing template, page 126
  (optional)

Palette, such as a plastic lid

Round brush, 1/8 to 1/4 inch (3 to 6 mm)

Stippling brush (optional)

Clear-gloss topcoat for exterior use

2 pieces of 1/2-inch (1.3 cm) yellow polyester
  rope, each approximately 11 feet
  (330 cm) long (If you use 2-inch [5.1 cm]
  board, use 3/4-inch [1.9 cm] rope.)

Matches or a lighter

WHAT YOU DO

1 Sand off any rough edges on the board.

2 On each end of the swing, measure in 1½ inches (3.8 cm) from the sides and edge, and mark the spot with a pencil.

3 Drill through the two marks to make holes for the rope. Start by drilling most of the way through on one side, then turn the board over and drill through from the opposite side, so you have a clean entrance on both sides.

4 With the flat brush, cover the entire board with primer. Brush primer inside the drilled holes as well. Let the primer dry.

5 Cover the entire board with dark green paint. Again, paint down into the holes, too. Let the paint dry.

6 Pour a small amount of lighter green paint onto wax paper, and use the sea sponge to sponge it over the dark green on the top and edges of the board. Let the paint dry.

7 Use the template to pencil daisies onto the board, or if you'd rather, free hand your flowers. Let the design extend onto the board's edges.

8 Use the round brush to fill in the petals with white paint. Let them dry.

9 In the palette, mix a little yellow paint with white, and brush a stroke on each petal, starting at the center of the petal and extending about two-thirds of the way down. Let the strokes dry.

10 With the stippling brush or sponge, mark the center of each flower with yellow paint, and let them dry.

11 Stipple or sponge a small amount of gold over the yellow centers. Let them dry.

12 Add water to a small amount of gold paint until it's a subtle wash of gold. Brush the wash on the petals, beginning at the center ends and brushing out the length of the petals, applying the wash more heavily at the center ends. Let the wash dry.

13 Dip the end of the round brush into the gold paint, and use it to scatter gold-dot accents on the board. Let them dry.

14 Brush or spray the clear-gloss topcoat over the entire board, including inside the drilled holes, to seal it and make it water-resistant. Let the topcoat dry.

15 With a match or a lighter, heat one end of each length of rope to make the ends easier to thread through the board's holes. Thread the heated ends through the holes in the board, and knot them securely on the bottom of the board.

how to hang your swing

1 Choose your tree and limb. Make sure the tree is healthy, and pick a limb that's as parallel to the ground as possible. If your tree is soft wood, such as cherry, you probably want a limb that's about 5 to 6 inches (12.7 to 15.2 cm) thick. With harder woods (oak, maple, etc.), your supporting limb can be as thin as 4 inches (10.2 cm) in diameter.

2 Attach the free ends of the rope to screw eyes, using a bowline knot. To tie a bowline knot, make a loop near the end of the rope, put the tail through the loop, bring it around the rope once, then through the loop once more. Pull tight.

3 Drill ¼-inch (6 mm) holes into the limb, making them as far apart as the holes in your swing seat.

4 Install the screw eyes into each hole in the limb.

MAKING A FIREFLY LANTERN

You need a clean glass jar with a screw-top lid, such as a mayonnaise jar, and a flat-head screwdriver or a hammer and a nail. Remove the lid and place it on a solid work surface. Pierce the lid several times with the sharp end of the screwdriver or nail, creating small openings for airflow. Grab a flashlight and wait for dark—and your chance to fuel your lantern with fireflies.

CATCHING FIREFLIES

Around dusk, turn off all exterior and interior lights. The darker it is, the easier it will be to locate fireflies by their tell-tale flashing. Mimic their signal patterns with your flashlight, shining it straight up or down, but not at the fireflies. They should fly over to your light. Gently catch them one by one with your hand, and place them in your lantern. It helps to have someone else holding the jar and twisting off the lid each time.

After enjoying your lantern for a short time, thank the fireflies for lighting up your life by setting them free.

FIREFLY FACTS

Also called lightning bugs, these luminous little creatures are winged nocturnal beetles found on every continent on earth. There are nearly 2,000 species, all members of the *Lampyridae* family. Their flashing lights are mating calls, distress beacons, and warning signals. Bioluminescence is the name for the process that makes fireflies light up; their "glow" colors range from yellow to red-orange to green. The flashing action of the light originates from the beetle's abdomen, where oxygen reacts with chemicals to produce light. Fireflies are completely harmless to humans, but their glow warns predators that they make for a toxic meal.

S INCE WELL BEFORE THE DAYS OF FIRECRACKERS and bottle rockets, human beings have been captivated by the blinking, twinkling, and much more mysterious pyrotechnics of the humble firefly. Here's how to rekindle the simple summer pleasure of sitting back and watching them glow.

ATTRACTING FIREFLIES

Fireflies abound on edges of woods and in fields. In your yard, they'll be attracted to low, overhanging trees, lush gardens, and tall grasses, where they can rest out of the sun during the day. You can make such a habitat even more firefly friendly by keeping it well hydrated; firefly larvae live either underwater, underground, or in humus, and feed on snails, slugs, and earthworms. (Most adult fireflies don't eat, though in some species, the adult female devours the male after mating.) You can also lure fireflies by reducing the lighting in and around your home, since they aren't competitive insects.

Fireflies: lighting up a summer night near you

school's out centerpiece

DESIGNER: **KENNETH TRUMBAUER**

So, you're old enough now that summer no longer means a three-month recess from the daily grind. You can still relive the spirit of those carefree times with this clever conversion of school lunch box into vase.

WHAT YOU NEED

Old metal lunch box

White trash bag

Scissors

Floral foam, a couple of blocks

Knife for cutting foam, if necessary

About 9 Gerbera daisies, mums, or
    other flowers with full, large heads
    in three different colors

Floral moss (optional)

WHAT YOU DO

1 Wipe the lunch box clean, and line it with plastic. Cut away the excess plastic.

2 Saturate the floral foam by floating it in a container of water, letting it absorb the moisture naturally. It's fully saturated when it sinks, and air bubbles stop rising to the surface. This usually takes about 30 minutes. Don't over-soak your foam, or it may disintegrate.

3 Fill the lunch box with tightly fitting pieces of foam.

4 Wash the flower stems and cut them to about a 3-inch (7.6 cm) length.

5 Stick the stems into the floral foam, arranging the flowers in three distinct colored rows or in a hopscotch pattern.

6 Fill any gaps between flowers with moistened moss.

lawn chair revival

DESIGNER: **DIANA LIGHT**

1940s-era metal chairs like these are everywhere today, popular for their back-to-the-past flair. (If you don't already have a couple tucked away in the garage, check flea markets and antique stores.) They're loaded with character, but also typically covered with rust and peeling paint. Here's how to bring back their charm and then some.

WHAT YOU NEED

Metal chair

Soap

Steel wool

Sandpaper

Mineral spirits

Old rags

Rust-control enamel paint in red and white

Flat nylon/polyester brush, 2 inches (5.1 cm)

Lawn Chair Revival template, page 126

Scissors

Tape

Pencil or ballpoint pen

Small detail brush

Medium round brush, about ¼ inch (6 mm)

Container for holding brushes and mineral spirits

WHAT YOU DO

1 With soap and steel wool, scrub the chair clean, as best you can, and let it dry.

2 Sand down any rust spots or chipping paint.

3 Wet a rag with mineral spirits, and wipe the chair.

4 Use the flat brush to cover the entire chair with red paint. Start by turning the chair upside down and painting the underside. When it's dry, turn it over and paint the top and sides. When it's dry, paint a second coat, if necessary, and let it dry again.

5 Cut the template into six pieces (five petals and the center), tape them to the inside back of the chair, and trace around them. Try not to tear through the paint, as you do.

6 Remove the template pieces and paint inside the outlines with white paint, using the small detail brush. It's easiest (and causes less dripping) to do this if you lay the chair on its back, so the area you're painting on is flat. Let the paint dry, and add a second coat, if necessary.

7 If you get white paint on areas meant to be red, clean them up with mineral spirits and a rag, or repaint them with red.

8 Clean your brushes with mineral spirits and then with soap and water.

REMEMBER BACK WHEN YARD WORK MEANT LITTLE MORE THAN SETTING UP A NET or sticking some metal hoops in the ground? Dig down past all the minutia about weeding and mulching that now fills your head, and remind yourself why you have a lawn in the first place.

BOCCE BALL

First played in Italy, bocce ball's popularity spread throughout Europe. It's rumored that Sir Francis Drake and Queen Elizabeth refused to interrupt their game, even as the invading Spanish Armada sailed across the English Channel. Bocce ball is played with four pairs of metal, tennis-sized balls—two for each player—and one smaller rubber ball. Throw the smaller ball out on the lawn. Then let players take turns rolling their balls toward the target ball. The player whose ball is nearest the rubber ball at the end of the game wins.

CROQUET

This game of balls, mallets, and hoops resembles golf. Push the metal hoops into the ground. Assign each player a colored ball and a mallet. As shots alternate, each player tries to get his or her ball through the first hoop. The first to do so wins a point. Then play moves to the next hoop. When all the hoops have been played, the person with the most points wins.

BADMINTON

Known for centuries by such names as "Battledore and Shuttlecock" and "Poona," badminton finally gained its official name (and rules) when it was played at a garden party held by the Duke of Beaufort at his country home, Badminton. To play, you need four things: two rackets, a shuttlecock (or birdie), a net, and one other player. Stand on opposite sides of the net in opposite corners. The first player serves, always underhand, and the play begins. If the shuttlecock hits the ground or goes out of bounds, the server scores a point or the receiver wins the serve. The first player to win 15 points wins the match.

ULTIMATE FRISBEE

This is a relatively recent yard game, probably because the Frisbee itself was invented a mere 50 years ago. The game was thought up by a group of high school students in New Jersey in 1967. While there are official rules, we encourage you to play the game according to the spirit in which it was invented—making it up as you go along. There are only two rules that really matter in Ultimate Frisbee: you can't run with the Frisbee and you can't touch the person holding the Frisbee. (Another helpful rule is known as the "10-second rule." If the person holding the Frisbee doesn't throw it in 10 seconds, the other team takes possession.) Divide into two teams, set up boundaries and end zones. Often, these are about the size of a soccer field, but the number and stamina of the players ultimately determine the size of the field. To score, pass the Frisbee from teammate to teammate and into the opposing team's end zone. The first team to reach an agreed-upon score wins.

Yard games

WHAT YOU NEED

Variety of four-wheeled metal wagons

Assorted cushions and pillows, approximately the same size as wagon interiors

Assorted small carpets and rag rugs

Wood shims or blocks

WHAT YOU DO

1 Arrange the wagons in a circle, so your guests can face each other, or in separate conversational groups if you prefer.

2 Fit the cushions into the wagon beds. Cover the cushions with carpets or rag rugs for extra comfort.

3 To stabilize the wagons, tuck wood shims or blocks between the bottom of the wheels and the ground.

DESIGNER: **ROB PULLEYN**

circle your wagons

The same little red wagon that once hauled a family of dolls, your lemonade-stand supplies, or the world's best dog—who always cheerfully endured the ride—can also play a part in grown-up summer games. Collect your own "fleet," then let one hold the chilled wine, another the cheese and fruit, and the rest serve as clever seating for an impromptu crowd.

S'more is more

LET'S HEAR IT FOR SENSORY MEMORY. At least since 1927, when the Girl Scouts printed the recipe for s'mores in their handbook, young campers everywhere have been happily smushing together this completely sweet, satisfyingly gooey, outdoorsy classic. And there's no sign most of us outgrow the taste.

Today, you can find ice cream studded with s'mores, s'more-style candies, and, at chichi restaurants where tabletop pots of coals stand in for campfires, everything from make-your-own gourmet s'mores (complete with glasses of port on the side) to nouveau s'more tarts. Does that put you in the mood for a round of "Kum-bay-ah," or what?

Here's the classic recipe you can riff on any way you like.

CAMPFIRE S'MORES

    8 sticks (for toasting
      the marshmallows)
   16 graham crackers
    8 bars plain chocolate,
      broken in two
   16 marshmallows

1 Toast two marshmallows over the coals of a campfire until they reach a crispy, gooey state.

2 Put them inside a graham-cracker-and-chocolate-bar sandwich.

3 Let the heat of the marshmallows between the halves of chocolate bar melt the chocolate a bit.

Yearning for a touch of the pseudo-Polynesian glamour of the tiki lounges of decades ago? These beaded torches are it. Stock the drink table with plenty of maraschino cherry garnishes, turn up the marimba music, and celebrate the return of tiki fever.

beaded tiki torches

DESIGNER: **DIANA LIGHT**

WHAT YOU NEED

Plain torches

Old coins with green patina (one per torch)

Wood beads in various sizes, shapes, and colors

Hemp cord in 1 mm and 3 mm sizes (about 1 yard [.9 m] per torch)

Wood animal beads (two per torch)

Simulated bone beads (two per torch)

Cyanoacrylate glue

Hot-glue gun and glue sticks

Jade beads (two per torch)

Scissors

WHAT YOU DO

1 Remove the metal insert cans from your torches to make them easier to work with.

2 Start with the 3 mm hemp cord. Make a knot about 9 inches (22.9 cm) in from the end. String on a large wood bead, knot the rope, string on a simulated bone bead, and knot the rope again.

3 Hold the beaded cord up to the torch, about one-third of the way down from the top. Wrap it around the torch, and tie a knot on the other side to correspond with the last knot you tied in step 2. String on a simulated bone bead, tie a knot, string on a large wood bead, and tie another knot.

4 Tie the ends of the cord together in a square knot at the center front of the torch. Pull firmly on the hemp, so it's snug on the torch.

5 Repeat steps 2 through 4 with the 1-mm cord, using smaller wood beads and varying the stringing pattern, if you like. If you end up with too much cord to tie it snugly around the torch, just tie a few extra knots in the back to shorten it.

6 Thread the 1-mm cord through the coin. With cyanoacrylate glue, attach the back of the coin to the center knot of the 3-mm cord, to help anchor the coin.

7 String more small wood beads and the animal and jade beads to the ends of the 1-mm cord. Use hot glue on the ends of the cord to anchor the last beads in place.

8 String a medium-size wood bead on each end of the 3 mm cord, and anchor each with hot glue.

9 Use hot glue to anchor the back of the square knot in the 3-mm cord to the torch.

set to memory

DESIGNER: **KENNETH TRUMBAUER**

start with what you have

The bright yellow cafeteria trays were the inspiration for this cheerful setting. They established the playful tone and even helped set the menu—their useful little sections are perfect for fondue tidbits and sauces. Other collectibles that could create a setting range from vintage linens and enamelware pitchers to antique soda bottles turned vases.

set a color scheme

You'll both unify your setting and sharpen the look if you limit the colors you incorporate. We went with the classic and summery combination of yellow and red, then added dashes of shiny silver.

fill in the gaps

Remember, you're doing this for fun, not historic accuracy. Feel free to mix pieces from different periods and to blend in modern items where you need them. We had the red metal garden chairs and small round table. To help the white kitchenette table fit in, we added a strip of red paint around the edge and an heirloom-print tablecloth on top. Tag-sale plastic glasses decorated with bits of old television trivia add an acceptable amount of kitsch, and the contemporary martini glasses work just fine, thanks to their whimsical design and colored bases.

Summer sends lots of us off into thoughts of simpler times, whether we actually experienced them or just wish we had. Give guests a taste of the bygone eras that capture your fancy by turning memorabilia and pieces of a vintage collection into a one-of-a-kind table setting.

PITCHER-PERFECT LEMONADE

    1 cup (.24 L) water
  1½ cups (300 g) sugar
15–18 medium lemons,
          to yield 3 cups (.72 L) of juice
    5 cups (1.2 L) cold water

■ Bring the water and sugar to boil in a saucepan, stirring occasionally, until the sugar dissolves.

■ Allow the syrup to cool.

■ Microwave five or six lemons at a time at a high power setting for 1 to 1½ minutes, until just warm to the touch. (Another option is to set your lemons out in the sun until they soften and warm.)

■ Cut the lemons in half and squeeze the juice into a pitcher.

■ Skim out the seeds, so you're left with only pulpy juice in the pitcher.

■ Repeat with the remaining lemons. Allow the juice to cool, then stir in the syrup and the rest of the water.

VARIATION: For pink lemonade, add ½ cup (.12 L) of cranberry juice.

Makes about 2 quarts (1.9 L).

Lemonade stand review

MAYBE IT WAS YOUR INTRODUCTION TO THE THRILL OF ENTREPRENEURSHIP. Or maybe you drank most of your profits, but had the time of your life anyway. Whichever, the curbside lemonade stand was, for many, the ultimate summertime right of passage. Here are the steps for helping a budding businessperson set one up.

1 LOCATION. Pick a strategic site. A corner with lots of foot traffic is ideal. Under a shady tree is best.

2 PRODUCT DEVELOPMENT. Decide what your stand will offer. Lemonade only, or will you sell limeade, too? See if others want to sell cookies, maybe, or handmade fans. Prepare the lemonade and other items.

3 MERCHANDISING. Calculate prices based on the cost of ingredients and materials. Don't forget cups, straws, napkins, and any extras.

4 ADVERTISING. Make a big, bright sign large enough to attract the attention of those in cars as well as pedestrians. Use descriptive terms such as "Ice Cold," "Fresh-Squeezed," and "Yum!" Recruit a sibling or friend to drum up business by putting up smaller signs around the neighborhood, telling where and when the stand will be open.

5 SETTING UP SHOP. You'll need a table for sure. A small ladder beside it gives you extra display space and can help hold supplies. You'll also need a jar or box with a lid for collecting money. Fill it with a handful of coins before you open, so you can make change for your first few customers. You'll probably want a cooler of ice, too. Instead of adding ice to the lemonade (it'll melt and make the lemonade watery), you can fill each cup with ice before you pour lemonade on top.

6 PRODUCT DISPLAY. Set out your wares. An inexpensive, clear cookie or apothecary jar makes a pretty container for lemonade. You can dip it out with a ladle. Small touches go a long way in making your stand special. Slice some lemon wedges, and have a bouquet of fresh sprigs of mint on the table, for example, to garnish the lemonade.

If you're lucky, making necklaces, anklets, and crowns of strung flowers was once as much a part of your summer as skipping rope and sprinting through the sprinkler. Indulge in a daisy chain session today, and you can use the same tried-and-true technique to create enchantingly simple garlands for everything from table runners to decorations for your front door. Here's a refresher on twisting together a chain.

DESIGNER: **SKIP WADE**

old-fashioned daisy chains

summer style

WHAT YOU NEED

Daisies (Other single-headed flowers that
    work well include pansies, poppies,
    buttercups, and wild clovers.)

Scissors

Florist's tape

WHAT YOU DO

1 Cut your flowers so you have stems of
about 6 inches (15.2 cm) to work with. If
you want a tighter chain, cut the stems
shorter. Just keep in mind you'll need a little
more dexterity to work with them.

2 Press the stems to flatten them, so
they're more pliable.

3 Begin by wrapping the stem of one
flower behind its head, then twist the end
around the stem several times.

4 Wrap a small piece of florist's tape
around the stem end to secure the twist.

5 Thread the stem of a new flower through
the loop of the first one, and continue until
you have a chain the length you need.

Fountain of youth

HOW CAN YOU FORGET THE DEADLINES, the to-do lists, and the electronic messages, and recapture a few moments of the good old days? Start with number one, and work your way down.

1 Run through a sprinkler.

2 Stage a three-legged race.

3 Have a water-balloon fight.

4 Lie on the grass and eat a Popsicle.

5 Sit on a blanket outside with a friend, and paint each other's toenails.

6 Climb a tree.

7 Start a diary.

8 Set up an obstacle course, then run it.

9 Go berry picking.

10 Eat a double-scoop ice cream cone.

11 Gather three friends and a piece of chalk, and play hopscotch.

12 Walk barefoot in the grass.

13 Pick a bouquet of wildflowers.

14 Take a bike ride.

15 Go skinny-dipping.

16 Eat a slice of watermelon and spit the seeds.

17 Drink an ice-cold soda in a glass bottle.

18 Do a few somersaults down a hill.

19 Squirt someone with a squirt gun.

20 Lie down on a blanket under a tree, and reread a favorite book.

21 Have a jump-rope contest.

22 Listen for the ocean in a seashell.

23 Ride a ferris wheel.

24 Spend the night in a tree house.

25 Kick your feet in a pool, creek, lake, pond, the ocean, or a wading pool.

In Bloom

Earth laughs in flowers...
—Ralph Waldo Emerson

3

SUMMER
STYLE

fun foam place settings

DESIGNER: **TERRY TAYLOR**

Precut pieces of craft foam, available in all sorts of floral and other shapes, make this happy project a snap. Tackle it after lunch, and you can still squeeze in a shift in the hammock before your new settings make their debut at dinner.

WHAT YOU NEED

12 x 18-inch (30.5 x 45.7 cm) sheets of craft foam (1 per place mat)

Precut craft foam shapes (If you have a special theme in mind and can't find shapes to match, go ahead and cut your pieces out of sheets of craft foam.)

White craft glue

Hole punch

Eyelets and eyelet punch

Scissors

WHAT YOU DO

1 Lay your craft shapes on the large foam sheets. Layer shapes on top of one another, if you like. Fiddle with the placement of the shapes until you're happy with the look, then glue them in place on the sheets. If you have a couple of heavy books around, place them on the shapes until they're dry.

2 Use the hole punch to make holes around the perimeter of the place mats. Use the eyelet punch to set an eyelet in each hole.

3 Make matching napkin rings with 1½ x 5-inch (6.4 x 12.7 cm) strips of craft foam. Glue the strips into rings, then add a decorative shape to top each off.

IF YOU'RE PICKING YOUR OWN

Try to harvest flowers in the early part of the day, before the sun zaps their internal water supply. Whatever the time, take a bucket of water with you, and plunge the stems in it immediately after cutting them. Choose flowers that aren't quite in full bloom; they'll last longer once they're cut. And leave new buds alone. They'll quickly become limp in a display, but left in place, they'll produce blooms for your next bouquet.

CUTTING

As soon as you get your flowers inside or home from the market, give all the stems a fresh cut on a diagonal. When they're placed in their container, the flowers will rest on the point of the cut rather than flat, leaving room for water to flow up the stem. Also, strip off any leaves that will be below the water line in the arrangement. Leaves submerged in water will rot quickly, and most flowers do better if they're not competing with their own foliage for water. At the same time, remove any damaged petals and snip off any thorns on the stems.

If you have time, let your recut flowers sit in a temporary container in a cool, dark place overnight, so they can take a good, long drink. This process, called hardening, ensures that the flowers absorb as much water as possible before they begin sealing off their pores.

FEEDING & WATERING

When you submerge your flower stems, whether to harden them overnight or for the final arrangement, use tepid water. It's easier for oxygen to travel through on its way up the stems. Adding floral food will nourish your flowers, encourage buds to develop, and help prevent bacteria from growing. You can mix your own by dissolving a capful of bleach and a couple of small spoonfuls of sugar in a gallon (3.8 L) of water. Most critical, however, is that you change the water regularly, keeping it clean and sparkling.

WE ASK A LOT OF CUT FLOWERS, expecting them to look perky and bright long after we've deprived them of their natural source of nutrients and water. The least we can do is help them adjust.

Fresh flowers
(and keeping them that way)

heirloom floral trays

DESIGNER: **DIANA LIGHT**

Swatches of tea-stained fabric give these serving trays their undeniable antique charm. They're handy for everything from setting out bowls of fresh berries and cream to delivering sundaes to a crowd.

WHAT YOU NEED

Unfinished wood nesting trays

Latex primer

Flat, 1-inch (2.5 cm) artist's brush

Ivory acrylic paint

Black tea

Floral fabric, 100 percent cotton

Sharp, precision-tip scissors

Matte decoupage medium

Acrylic paints in colors to match the flowers on your fabric

Small round artist's brush

Ruler

Pencil

WHAT YOU DO

1 Using the flat brush, cover your trays completely with a coat of latex primer. Let them dry.

2 Cover the trays again with a coat of ivory paint.

3 Make a pot of black tea, and soak the fabric in it to "age" it. Check the fabric every minute or so to see if it has colored enough. When you're satisfied, remove the fabric and let it dry.

4 Carefully cut the flower images out of the fabric, and place them how you want them on the insides of the trays. Let the flowers overlap onto the inner sides of the trays.

5 Using the flat brush again, apply decoupage medium where each flower will be, then pat the flowers in place and let them dry.

6 With the round brush and the colored paints, add accents such as stems and polka dots to the insides of the trays. An easy way to make dots is to use the end of the handle of the brush.

VARIATION: To add stripes to one of your trays, like the ones on the purple tray shown here, before you add the flowers, use the ruler and pencil to lay down stripe lines. Paint them and let them dry, then decoupage the flowers in place.

7 Use the pencil to lightly draw curlicues or other accents on the outside edges of the trays. Paint the accents and let them dry.

8 Brush decoupage medium over all the trays. The outsides will need only one coat; give the insides at least three coats.

Shopping farmer's markets

SUMMER IS UNDENIABLY ABOUT THE BOUNTY OF VEGETABLE GARDENS, fruit orchards, herb beds, and berry patches, and it's never been easier to partake, even if your own agricultural ambitions stop with the jade plant on your windowsill. Local farmers' markets—think of them as convenient and festive conventions of small roadside fruit and vegetable stands—are thriving in towns and cities around the world. Producers show up in person to vend enticing items they've grown, reared, caught, picked, brewed, pickled, baked, smoked, or otherwise made themselves. Here's how to make the most of a market near you.

LOOK FOR A LISTING. If there are farmers' markets in your area, a schedule should appear on the calendar page of the local newspaper and/or on community bulletin boards. They're also sometimes referred to as tailgate markets. In addition to shopping your hometown market, finding a nearby farmers' market can be a wonderful way to get to know the place where you're spending your summer vacation.

SHOP EARLY. Favorite items—blueberries, homemade salsa, oyster mushrooms—move fast. The earlier you go, the better, in terms of both availability and selection. Of course, if part of the attraction of these events for you is bargaining for good deals, go just before the market ends, when vendors are often happy to haggle.

SKIP THE LIST. It's fine to go with an intention to buy some specific items (salad greens for that night's dinner party, eggs for the next morning's brunch), but don't be too focused. The old-fashioned fun of farmers' markets is in searching out the freshest and best-looking ingredients, then planning your meals around them.

BROWSE FIRST. Stroll, survey, and taste test (lots of vendors set out samples or slice them up on request) before you buy. Get the lay of the land, then go back and make your purchases. Once you're familiar with a particular market, you'll know that you want to head first for the stall with the good arugula or the heirloom apples.

BRING A BAG. Or a basket or a small rolling cart. Farmers' markets typically don't provide shopping carts.

TAKE SMALL BILLS AND CHANGE. The charm of these places is that they don't feature cash machines and electronic registers. Vendors are typically prepared with several rolls of coins and their own stack of small bills, but you'll add to the ease of your transactions if you can come close to giving them correct change.

CHAT, SOCIALIZE, SIP. Take your coffee with you, or buy some on site. Catch up with friends and neighbors. Best of all, talk with vendors. Meeting the real live people behind the produce is one of the biggest benefits of a farmers' market. They can tell you several good ways to cook their Chioggia beets, offer tips on transplanting their perennials, and give you a bit of family lore to go with their homemade strawberry-rhubarb jam. Once vendors get to know you and your preferences, they'll often also be willing to set items aside for you each week.

DESIGNER: **ALLISON SMITH**

garden catalog coasters

It's a well-known fact among flower fanatics: Even urban dwellers without a patch of soil love luxuriating in the lush, vibrant pages of garden catalogs. Here's a clever way to enjoy the blooms they feature all summer, whether you ever plant a seed or not.

WHAT YOU NEED

Several sheets of vellum

Circle-cutting tool or a protractor

Scissors

Garden catalogs

Small tacky glue stick

Clear peel-and-stick laminating sheets

Credit card or craft stick

WHAT YOU DO

1 Use the circle-cutting tool or a protractor and scissors to cut 4-inch (10.2 cm) circles out of the sheets of velum, one circle per coaster.

2 Cut large, round flowers out of the garden catalog with scissors. Cut out the detailed edges of all the flower petals.

3 Use a very small dot of glue to secure each flower to a velum circle. The idea is not to actually glue the flowers down, but to hold them in place until they're laminated.

4 Place a sheet of laminate face down on a flat surface, and carefully remove the paper backing. Place the velum circles with flowers on top, flowers facing down.

5 Peel the paper backing off the edge of a second sheet of laminate. Stick the exposed edge down onto the edge of the first piece. Using one slow motion, continue peeling off the backing as you smooth down the laminate.

6 Use a credit card or the side of a craft stick to smooth the laminate.

7 Trim away the excess laminate from your coasters.

pressed flower candle

Flowers and candlelight make a pretty good pair any time of year. This especially summery spin on the combination can serve as table light and centerpiece in one.

DESIGNER: **DIANA LIGHT**

WHAT YOU NEED

Triple-wick candle in ivory

Old pair of nylons

Dried pressed flowers

Craft glue

Small artist's brush

Gloss decoupage medium

Flat artist's brush, about 1 to 1½ inches (2.5 to 3.8 cm)

TIP: It's best to gather flowers you plan to press during midday. Press them in a heavy book for a couple of weeks.

WHAT YOU DO

1 Use the old nylons to buff the candle all over, smoothing out scratches and other marks.

2 Arrange your pressed flowers on the candle in a design that pleases you. Here, they're mimicking flowers growing up out of the ground.

3 With the small brush, carefully apply glue to the backs of the flowers, and press them into place. Let them dry.

4 With the larger brush, apply decoupage medium in vertical strokes from the top to the bottom of the candle. Wipe off any excess decoupage medium at either end. Apply three coats, letting each coat dry completely before adding another. Don't decoupage the top of the candle.

TEN IDEAS each for dealing with bushel baskets of tomatoes and zucchini.

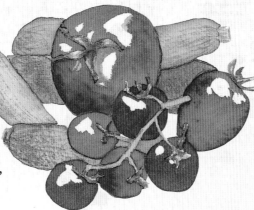

TOMATOES

1 **SALSA.** Toss tomato chunks with diced chili peppers, onions, and garlic. Add a little salt, pepper, olive oil, lime juice, and fresh cilantro.

2 **BRUSCHETTA.** Cut a loaf of crusty white bread into slices. Spread a thick layer of goat cheese on each slice. Top with chopped tomatoes, garlic, and basil mixed with olive oil. Broil the slices until they're warm.

3 **SUN-DRIED TOMATOES.** Well, okay, oven-dried. Cut your tomatoes into slices. Put the slices on foil-lined cookie sheets, and dry them in a warm oven for 10 to 24 hours. Store them in airtight containers or in olive oil.

4 **BROILED TOMATOES.** Peel and cut tomatoes into halves or thick slices. Place them on a broiler pan and put them in an oven. When the tomato halves are hot, brush them with butter and season them with salt, pepper, and herbs. Broil them until they're brown and serve them hot.

5 **BAKED TOMATOES.** Halve some tomatoes, cover them with bread crumbs, and bake them until they're brown.

6 **FRIED GREEN TOMATOES.** Cut a large green tomato into thin slices. Sprinkle a pinch of sugar on each slice. Coat the slices with flour, and fry them over medium heat until they're golden brown.

7 **TOMATO OMELET.** Add fresh basil and mozzarella for an Italian version. Jalapeños and Monterey jack cheese make it Mexican.

8 **TOMATO FRIES.** Peel and slice well-ripened tomatoes. Dust them with sugar. Dip each slice in thick pancake batter. Fry at a medium heat until brown. Serve with spicy mustard.

9 **STUFFED TOMATOES.** Remove about two-thirds of the pulp from a tomato. Mix it with some precooked rice, couscous, quinoa, bulgur wheat, or grits. Add salt and pepper, chopped celery and parsley, and cheese or precooked meat such as crumbled sausage or cubes of chicken, if you like. Fill the hollowed-out tomato with the mixture. Cover with well-buttered bread crumbs and bake at 350°F (180°C) for about 20 minutes.

VARIATION: Stuff the tomato with finely chopped corn or even creamed corn, and bake it in the oven until brown. This is a wonderful substitute for a baked potato.

10 **TOMATO-AND-MAYONNAISE SANDWICH.** Make this classic on fluffy white bread with a bibb lettuce leaf.

ZUCCHINI

1 **ZUCCHINI BREAD.** Sort of like banana bread, but better tasting and better for you.

2 **ZUCCHINI STIR-FRY.** Sliced thinly, zucchini is a great addition to any concoction in a wok.

3 **ZUCCHINI PICKLES.** Make them just like bread-and-butter pickles. They taste like candy.

4 **CHOCOLATE ZUCCHINI CAKE.** Drop "zucchini" from the name, and see if anyone can guess what the mystery ingredient is.

5 **ZUCCHINI SOUP.** Try it cold on really hot days.

6 **ZUCCHINI SALAD.** Slice and steam the zucchini, and toss it with steamed red potatoes (sliced), olive oil, and lemon juice.

7 **ZUCCHINI KEBAB.** Skewer pieces of zucchini and grill them with any other summer veggies you have.

8 **ZUCCHINI GIFT BASKETS.** Give them away to non-gardening neighbors and friends.

9 **ZUCCHINI BOAT.** If you've grown a zucchini so large it's inedible, cut it in half, hollow out the inside, and use it as container for dip, raw veggies, or salad.

10 **SQUASH TOSS.** Take a bunch out to a wide-open space, and see who can throw his or her zucchini the farthest.

If all else fails, nip it in the bud. Put a stop to propagation by removing the female zucchini blossoms (those attached to the stem with a bulge).

Bumper crop coping mechanisms

giant hibiscus glamour cushions

DESIGNER: **JANE WILSON**

Whether you need an inexpensive substitute for a tropical vacation or have a burning desire to drape yourself dramatically over something soft, a few of these luscious, oversize throws is your answer. They're also perfect, scattered around as seating, for a spur-of-the-moment luau.

WHAT YOU NEED

Tape measure or ruler

Pencil, chalk, or fabric marker

½ yard (.45 m) textured, sheer fabric for
draperies, 45-inch (114.3 cm) width, in red,
pink, or white, for the flower stamens

Scissors

Straight pins

Thread in colors to match the stamens,
petals, and bract

Sewing machine

1 piece of crib quilt batting, 45 x 60 inches
(114.3 x 152.4 cm)

1 yard (.9 m) lining fabric, 45-inch
(114.3 cm) width

1 yard (.9 m) polyester fabric, 45-inch
(114.3 cm) width, in red, pink,
or maroon for the flower petals

Fine-tip permanent marker

Crochet hook or chopstick (optional)

Dressmaker's carbon paper (optional)

Tracing wheel (optional)

¼ yard (.23 m) fabric in dark green for
the flower bract

Upholstery needle

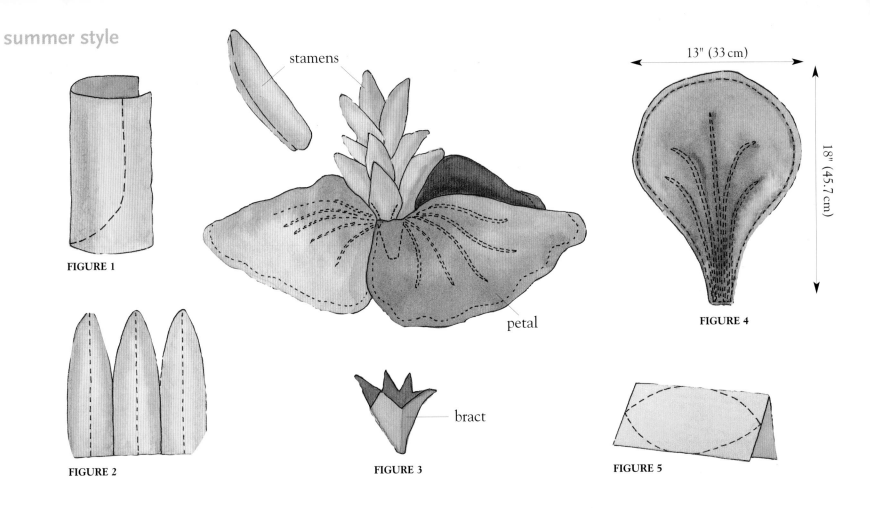

stamens

petal

bract

FIGURE 1

FIGURE 2

FIGURE 3

FIGURE 4

FIGURE 5

13" (33 cm)

18" (45.7 cm)

WHAT YOU DO

1 First, you'll make the "stamens" that form the center section of the pillow. Use the tape measure and pencil to measure and mark the drapery sheer in the following pieces: five 3 x 5-inch (7.6 cm x 12.7 cm) pieces, three 3 x 9-inch (7.6 x 22.9 cm) pieces, and three 3 x 12-inch (7.6 x 30.5 cm) pieces. Cut them out.

2 Fold the 3-inch (7.6 cm) side of each cutout piece in half as shown in figure 1, right side in, and pin the sides together. Use the pencil to lightly trace a shape on the fabric like the one in the illustration.

3 Thread the sewing machine, and use it to sew a ¼-inch (6 mm) seam along the outline you traced on the fabric, leaving the end open. Use the scissors to trim the seam, cutting a diagonal on the corner and small notches along the curve. Be careful not to cut into the seam.

4 Refer to figure 2. Turn the sewn pieces right side out. Lay the 5-inch-long (12.7 cm) pieces flat on the work surface, centering the seam on top as shown. Use the machine to sew together the pieces, seaming together only about half of their straight side edges and leaving the top, curved sections free. Repeat steps 2 through 4 to make the 9-inch (22.9 cm) and 12-inch-long (30.5 cm) groups of stamens, varying the length of the material accordingly.

5 Nest the three groups of stamens with the longest in the middle, surrounded by the mid-length stamens, and the shortest on the outside (see figure 3). Set aside.

6 Now you'll make the hibiscus petals. Enlarge the petal template in figure 4 to the dimensions indicated on the template. Make note of where you'll leave an opening on the seam.

7 Stack two layers of batting, a layer of lining, two layers of the polyester fabric turned right side in, and a layer of lining.

8 Lay the petal template on top and use the marker to trace around it, being sure to mark an opening for turning the petal right side out later. Remove the template. Pin the layers together and cut them out, leaving extra material around the edges so you can add a ½-inch (1.3 cm) seam allowance around the traced outline. Make a total of five cut-out petal "stacks."

9 Thread the sewing machine, set it to eight stitches per inch (2.5 cm), and sew a seam directly on the traced outline of each petal. Don't sew the opening closed. Trim the seam allowance to ¼ inch (6 mm), cutting the corners on the diagonal and cutting tiny notches in the curved seam allowance. Be careful not to cut into the seam.

10 Use your hands to open up the petal slightly at the opening, between the two layers of polyester fabric. Sew the polyester fabric on the bottom layer to the batting on the bottom, sewing along the edge of the opening. Do not sew the opening closed.

11 Turn the petal right side out through the opening you left in the seam. Use the crochet hook to poke out the corners if necessary. The petal will have a side that doesn't show the inner seams prominently; this will be the "face" of the petal. Position the template over the petal, and use the carbon paper and tracing wheel, if you like, to mark the quilting lines in the center and perimeter of the petal.

12 With the machine set to eight stitches per inch, machine-stitch a ¼-inch (6 mm) seam around the petal as marked on the template. Turn the raw edges of the opening you left in the seam allowance to the inside, being sure to run the quilting seam close enough to close the opening. Sew along the quilting lines, too.

13 Place the edges of two petals face together, and sew their two edges together by hand at their inner ends and midpoint. Use shallow stitches that join the fabric but not the batting. Continue to join the sides of the petals until they form a cup.

14 To make the "bract" that holds the lower ends of the petals underneath the flower, fold the forest green fabric right side together, and cut out five shapes as shown in figure 5. With the green thread in the machine, sew a ¼-inch (6 mm) seam along the curved edges, leaving an opening to turn them right side out. Trim the seam and corners, and turn each piece right side out. Use the green thread in the machine to sew the openings closed and to sew the lower edges of the bract components together, forming a cup shape.

15 Fit the stamens into the center of the sewn-together petal cup, and slide the bract over the bottom. Use the upholstery needle and green thread to sew all the pieces together at the bottom. The finished pillow will measure about 30 inches (76.2 cm) across, with a circumference of about 90 inches (228.6 cm).

IF SUMMER HAD AN OFFICIAL FRUIT, CHANCES ARE IT WOULD BE THE MELON. Some might lobby briefly for strawberries, blueberries, or peaches, but eventually, everyone would admit that melons, with their honey-flavored juice and delicate pastel-hued flesh, represent the essence of the sunlit season.

In the spirit of summer, melons are also obligingly flexible. They're happy to assume the form of cubes for salads, balls for garnishes, slush for smoothies, and slices to be eaten all by themselves. And they're the ultimate in summer-weather nutrition. Melons are one of the world's fastest-digested foods, an important feature on hot days, when much of your body's energy goes to cooling you down, and they're a water-saturated food, so they help keep you hydrated.

CANTALOUPE AND THEN SOME

Branch out, and you can find everything from melons shaped like snakes to melons that taste like mangos. Here's a guide to some of the more exotic varieties sold by specialty growers.

AMBROSIA. Ambrosia melons look and taste like a cantaloupe, but their flesh is brighter orange, making them a brilliant addition to fruit salad.

CANARY. The canary is a small oval melon with bright yellow skin and white flesh. Make sure it's ripe before you eat it, or the flesh will be very bland.

CHARENTAIS. A traditional French muskmelon, charentais is in the family of round, smooth-skinned melons that includes cantaloupes. The charentais has deep orange flesh and a honey flavor.

CRENSHAW. The dark green skin of a crenshaw melon turns yellow when it's ripe. The flesh is salmon colored.

KHARBOOZEH MASHEDI. Orange and yellow skin and flesh, and a taste some compare to that of an aged Chardonnay. It gets better. The ancient Persians considered this one an aphrodisiac.

KIWANO. Also known as the *African horned cucumber*, the *English tomato*, the *hedged gourd*, or the *jelly melon*, the kiwano has a spiky orange rind. Its yellow-green flesh has the consistency of jelly and tastes a bit like a cucumber.

MEDITERRANEAN. The Mediterranean melon is actually a somewhat large group of melons. It's also known as the *galia*, or Middle Eastern melon. Most have yellow skin when mature, with a sweet, aromatic white or light-green flesh.

OGEN. Commercially developed in kibbutz Ha-Ogen in Israel, the ogen is also called an Israeli melon. It's one of the smaller melons in the cantaloupe family. It has green skin with orange grooves and green flesh.

SANTA CLAUS. The Santa Claus has elongated, wrinkled, dark-green skin sporting darker green flecks and deliciously sweet white flesh.

SHARLYN. Similar in appearance to a cantaloupe, this melon with yellow-orange skin and creamy pink-white flesh has a sweet vanilla-cinnamon flavor.

SNAKE. Originally from Armenia, the unusual snake melon looks and tastes like a cucumber.

TIGER BABY. The tiger baby is a small, round watermelon with a flavor slightly reminiscent of cola.

PICKING A MELON

Avoid melons that have cracks, dents, or bruises. Don't worry about the *couche*, though. That's the part of the melon that was next to the ground as it grew. It's usually discolored and flattened.

Melons that are rounder and more symmetrical generally taste better.

If you're picking an aromatic melon, such as a cantaloupe or muskmelon, choose one that smells sweet; the stronger the smell, the better the melon.

Pick up melons to test their weight; they should be heavy for their size. Most melons are more than 90 percent water.

Test for ripeness by thumping on melons. Hold your dominant hand as if you were going to knock on a door. Deliver two or three good thumps to the round side of the melon. The melon is ripe if the sound is deep and thick. If it sounds hollow, it's not yet ready to eat.

CANTALOUPE WATER

1 cantaloupe, peeled, seeded, and cubed
Sugar to taste
6 cups (1.5 L) water

1 Put the cantaloupe, sugar, and 2 cups (.5 L) of the water in a blender. Blend until smooth.

2 Strain the mixture into a large pitcher

3 Add the remaining water, and stir well. Refrigerate until you're ready to serve. Stir the mixture before serving.

LEMON WATERMELON SMOOTHIE

1½ cups (approx. 340 g) seeded watermelon, diced
1 small container of lemon sorbet
8–10 ice cubes
1 tablespoon (15 mL) fresh lemon juice

Place all the ingredients in a blender, and blend on high until smooth. For an extra kick, add a shot of vodka or rum before you blend.

Serves 2

WATERMELON SORBET

Half of a medium watermelon, sliced lengthwise
1 small can frozen pink lemonade concentrate, thawed and undiluted
1 large can crushed pineapple, undrained
Sugar to taste
Fresh mint sprigs for garnish

1 Scoop out the watermelon flesh and put it in a blender or food processor. Process it until it's smooth.

2 Pour the puree through a strainer into a bowl, discarding pulp and any seeds.

3 Measure out 8 cups (2 L) of juice. Add the lemonade concentrate, pineapple, and sugar. Stir until the sugar dissolves.

4 Pour the mixture into a 13 x 9-inch (33 x 22.9 cm) pan. Cover it with plastic wrap and freeze until it's firm.

5 Break the frozen mixture into chunks. Place half of it back in the blender or food processor, and process until it's smooth. Repeat with the second half. Garnish and serve.

Use wild ferns, clippings from the ivy that's creeping up your trellis, even sprigs from an overgrown house plant to create this fresh green table cover and matching napkins. They'll give any meal a garden-party air.

DESIGNER: **DIANA LIGHT**

botanical-print napkins & tablecloth

WHAT YOU DO

Before you start, prewash the tablecloth and napkins to remove any sizing.

napkins

1 Measure in about 3½ inches (8.9 cm) from the sides of the napkins, and apply masking tape, so you mask the edges of a center square on each.

2 Pour some gold paint onto a sheet of wax paper, and use the sea sponge to fill in the squares. Pull up the tape and let the squares dry.

3 Lay a plant clipping out on another sheet of wax paper. Fill your palette with the three shades of green paint, and use the brush to apply the paints to the clipping. Work quickly; these paints dry fast.

4 Lay the clipping, paint side down, on a napkin. Cover it with clean sheets of wax paper, and roll the brayer over it. Be sure to hold the paper down as you roll, so it doesn't slip and smear the paint.

5 Continue this process to cover the napkin with plant stamps, letting some of the plants run off the napkins edges, then repeat the process with the other napkins.

6 After you've stamped all the napkins, gently brush some gold highlights onto the stamps. Also, add some subtle green highlights to some of the leaves.

7 Follow the instructions on your paint bottles about drying time and/or heat setting for permanency.

tablecloth

1 Mask and sponge a border around the edge of your tablecloth.

2 Stamp the tablecloth with plants, as you did the napkins, but leave the center of the cloth plain.

WHAT YOU NEED

Plain cloth tablecloth and napkins

Ruler

Masking tape

Fabric paints or acrylic paints and textile medium in gold and at least three shades of green

Wax paper

Sea sponge

Plant clippings

Palette

½-inch (1.3 cm) flat brush

Brayer

Rinse cup

Paper towels

Plastic or paper to protect work area

Gathering

Twas a balmy summer evening
and a goodly crowd was there.

— Hugh Antoine D'Arcy

SUMMER
STYLE

polka dot tablecloth & napkins

DESIGNER: **ALLISON SMITH**

The bright, bold look of batik is just what you need to make your table setting say summer. But to get the real thing, there's all that work of waxing and multiple rounds of dying. Here's a simpler, quicker method using photo-reactive paint. It gives you the style you want, but on a summertime schedule.

WHAT YOU NEED

Large disposable plastic drop cloth

Masking tape

Photo-reactive paint in red and yellow

3 large plastic containers

White tablecloth and napkins,
    100 percent cotton

3 medium sponge paintbrushes

100 metal washers in different sizes

100 pennies

WHAT YOU DO

Note: Before you begin, make sure you have a block of time when you can work uninterrupted. The paint can develop quickly, so you'll need to be available to monitor it.

1 Set up your work spot outside in the brightest direct sunlight possible. Spread out the plastic drop cloth and tape it down to a flat surface, such as your driveway or a large piece of plywood.

2 Dilute the photo-reactive paint with water, according to the packaging directions, in two of the plastic containers. Fill the third plastic container with water.

3 Start with the napkins first, so you can build your comfort level before moving onto the tablecloth. Spread a napkin out on the work surface, and paint it with water to wet it thoroughly.

4 Working quickly, paint three or four long red "S" lines on the napkin.

5 Paint in between the red lines with yellow paint. Blend the yellow paint into the red to create color variations of orange. Add a little more red if you like, but a little goes a long way. Continue blending until you achieve the color variation you want.

6 Immediately place the washers and coins on the napkin in a random pattern.

7 Let the napkin sit undisturbed in the sun for 15 minutes to one hour, until the pattern develops.

8. Repeat the process with the remaining napkins and the tablecloth. You can work on several at a time, as long as you have enough washers and coins on hand.

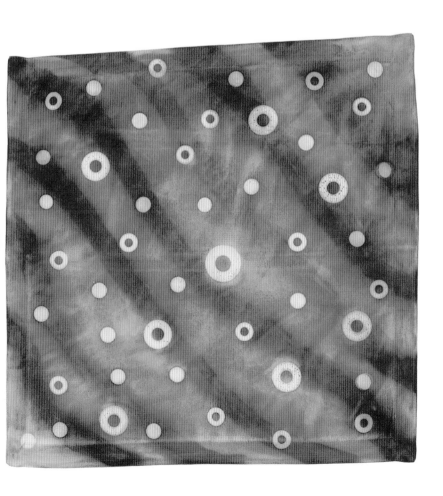

Chili-roasted corn for a crowd

HERE'S AN EASY WAY to add some zip to corn cooked on the grill.

Fresh ears of corn
Lime
Butter
Sea salt
Chili powder
Ice cubes

1 Shuck the corn. Place the ears in pairs on pieces of foil. Fold up the edges of the foil, so the corn doesn't roll around.

2 Place a slice of lime and a pat of butter on each ear of corn. Sprinkle each with sea salt and chili powder.

3 Put two ice cubes on each pair of corn, and fold the foil into a packet.

4 Place the packets of corn onto a covered grill, keeping them off direct heat. Cook about 15 or 20 minutes.

glass markers

DESIGNER: **ALLISON SMITH**

When people are mingling their way from pool to deck to patio and back, they may temporarily misplace what's theirs. These classy little tags are designed to help everyone tell their own wine, piña colada, or fruit punch from another's.

WHAT YOU NEED

Small glass beads
Metal charms
Large hand-blown glass beads
Plate covered with a towel
Medium metal earring hoops (one per marker)
Small pliers
Earring shanks
Wire cutters

WHAT YOU DO

1 Lay out a pattern of small glass beads on the towel-covered plate. Use a charm in the center of the pattern.

2 Once you're satisfied with the design, slip the beads and the charm onto a metal hoop.

3 With the pliers, bend the end tip of the hoop at a 90° angle to prevent the beads from slipping off.

4 Assemble as many more markers as you need, making every one a slightly different variation on the overall theme.

VARIATION: Instead of charms, use large hand-blown glass beads in the center of your markers. Lay out the beads as described above, and thread them onto an earring shank. With the pliers, bend the shank at a 90° angle just above the top bead. Cut the excess wire to 1/4 inch (6 mm). Firmly grab the end of the wire, and twist it back over itself to make a small circle.

flowers
on ice

DESIGNER: **KENNETH TRUMBAUER**

In the more casual, less disciplined season of summer, flowers are perfectly content to settle into all kinds of nontraditional containers, making it easy to tailor your bouquet to your gathering. Here, an art deco ice bucket stands in splendidly as a cocktail party vase. We filled it with snowball mums. Following is a list of other ideas for flower containers that suit a variety of summer styles.

OTHER SUMMER STYLE CONTAINERS:

Sand pails

Watering cans

Galvanized tubs

Olive oil, vinegar, and imported water bottles

Tropical juice cans

Old milk bottles in an antique carrier

Hollowed-out stalks of bamboo

Ceramic garden urns (Outdoor pots are typically porous and have a drainage hole in the bottom, so to turn them into containers for fresh flowers, you need to insert a vase inside the body.)

Clear glass sundae cups (Float a single blossom in each.)

Large cans with bright labels (Mexican coffee, imported tomatoes, etc.)

Champagne buckets

S UMMER FESTIVALS BEGAN AS PARTIES in honor of the season's best assets: long days, warm temperatures, and plentiful crops and game. You be the judge of whether too many hours in the sun inspired some of these events.

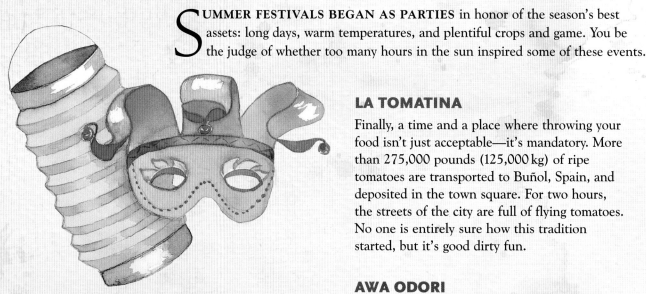

GREAT CARDBOARD BOAT REGATTA

Could you make a boat out of corrugated cardboard and row it for 600 yards (540 m)? This unusual race began as a final exam for design students at the University of Illinois in 1974. Since then, people throughout the United States have built and raced cardboard boats. Although grades are no longer given out, the most coveted prize is still the Titanic Award, given to the boat that sinks most spectacularly.

THE DRAGON BOAT FESTIVAL

In ancient China, the poet Qu Yan drowned himself in a river, protesting his government. People immediately rushed to their boats to search for him. Today, the Dragon Boat Festival commemorates this event, with boat races and feasts. Long ago, it was considered a good omen if a boat capsized during the race and someone drowned. Luckily, modern Chinese have jettisoned this tradition.

LA TOMATINA

Finally, a time and a place where throwing your food isn't just acceptable—it's mandatory. More than 275,000 pounds (125,000 kg) of ripe tomatoes are transported to Buñol, Spain, and deposited in the town square. For two hours, the streets of the city are full of flying tomatoes. No one is entirely sure how this tradition started, but it's good dirty fun.

AWA ODORI

In 1587, a Japanese feudal overlord threw a huge party to celebrate the completion of his castle. Everyone got drunk and danced around. The next morning (well, probably afternoon), they decided that it was so much fun they should do it every year. The traditional dance performed at the festival is called "The Dance of the Fools"; it mimics the drunken dance moves of the original party guests.

THE GREAT CHEESE ROLL

What began as a fertility rite 200 years ago in England is now a breakneck race down a steep hill chasing a 7½-pound (3.4 k) wheel of rolling cheese. The cheese can reach speeds of 34 mph (54.4 km)—faster than anyone can run. Contestants hurl themselves in front of the cheese in desperate attempts to stop it. (One year, 24 competitors, seven bystanders, and two emergency medical personnel were injured.) The winner takes home the cheese.

Official celebrations of summer

MIDNIGHT SUN BASEBALL GAME

In the latest baseball game ever, the first pitch is thrown at 10:35 p.m. This game is played entirely without artificial lights. It takes place in Fairbanks, Alaska, on the summer solstice.

THE GREAT MIGRATION

The world's most dangerous summer road trip is taken not by people, but by wildebeests, zebras, and gazelles. Each year, approximately a million of them begin moving west and north when the rain on the Serengeti grasslands dries up, usually sometime in May or June. By sometime between late July and early September, they reach Masai Mara, in Kenya, about 1,500 miles (2,400 km) away.

THE COASTER CON

Five thousand roller coaster aficionados (members of the ACE, American Coaster Enthusiasts) go on an annual road trip in search of the best roller coasters around. After an amusement park closes to regular customers, the ACE members get in line and start riding the roller coasters, competing to see who can stay on the longest.

WORLD BOG SNORKELING CHAMPIONSHIP

Contestants don wet suits, snorkels, masks, and fins for their race through the Waen Rhydd peat bog in Wales. During the race's two 60-yard (54 m) loops, you're allowed to pop your head up out of the bog only four times.

NUDE NIGHT SURFING CONTEST

In Sydney, Australia, this contest is exactly what it sounds like. Male contestants outnumber females by about four to one. The contest is broadcast via video to nearly 40 countries.

WORLD CHAMPIONSHIP COCKROACH RACES

In Brisbane, Australia, all you need to do is grab a cockroach, give it a good racing name, and join in the fun.

HOMOWO

To celebrate the harvest about to be gathered, people in Accra, Ghana, have a "Hunger Hooting" celebration. The roots of the festival go back hundreds of years to a great famine, when people hooted at the gods until the famine broke.

And, when you've finally had enough:

NATIONAL HERMIT WEEK

Celebrate a week of solitude in June. Close your shutters, turn off the phone, lock the door, and retreat to a shady spot in the backyard to be all by yourself. (In the U.S., this retreat appears on calendars during the second week of June, but you can declare your own hermitage anytime.)

Deconstructing summer whites

'TIS THE SEASON FOR PAIRING CHARDONNAY with poached salmon and Pinot Blanc with Thai green curry. Since at least half your guests are bound to bring a bottle of white wine to contribute to whatever's on the menu, why not suggest this most grown-up of drinking games? (It could even qualify as a tasting.) Simply photocopy the breakdown below, pass copies around, then let guests identify which of the classic white-wine characteristics they smell or taste in the glass they're sipping. If you really want to go all out, assemble some of the fruits, flowers, and other items listed on a tray, so guests can use them as a reference. Compare, contrast, and add to the list.

FRUIT
Apple
Apricot
Banana
Cherry
Grapefruit
Kiwi
Lemon
Lime
Melon
Peach
Pineapple

FLOWERS
Geranium
Lilac
Orange blossom
Rose
Violet

MINERALS, METALS, ROCK
Chalk
Flint
Lime
Slate
Steel

NUTS
Almond
Hazelnut
Pine nut
Pistachio
Walnut

SYRUP
Butter
Butterscotch
Honey

VEGETATION
Artichoke
Asparagus
Bell pepper
Fresh-cut grass
Green olive
Mint
Hay/straw

WOODY SPICE
Burned toast
Oak
Musty earth
Vanilla

gathering

Summer buffet-goers have their hands full. When they reach the end of the food table, they can't juggle lots of place-setting paraphernalia. These handy packs consolidate flatware, napkin, and place mat together into pretty, portable bundles. Guests can easily carry them off to the picnic table or a spot on the lawn.

WHAT YOU DO

1 Cut the Irish linen into an 18-inch (45.7 cm) section. Hem all the edges with a ¼-inch (6 mm) seam allowance.

2 Measure the width of the place mat. Add 9 inches (22.9 cm) to the measurement, and cut the grosgrain ribbon to this length. Also, cut a 9-inch (22.9 cm) piece of ribbon.

3 Measure 5 inches (12.7 cm) up from the bottom of the place mat. Working from right to left, pin the ribbon to the place mat at this point. On the right edge, fold the ribbon under itself about ⅜ inch (9.5 mm) to hide the raw edge. At the left edge, fold the ribbon under in the same way. Additional length of ribbon will extend past this edge; it will serve as half the tie.

4 Sew the ribbon to the place mat at both edges. When you sew the left edge, slip the 9-inch (22.9 cm) piece of ribbon you cut in step 2 under the first ribbon's folded edge, and sew it in place, too. Make pockets to fit the napkin and flatware by sewing additional seams (two on the right for the knife and spoon, and two on the left for the fork and napkin).

5 Trim the ends of the ribbon extending from the place mat's left edge, and treat them with fray retardant.

6 Tuck the flatware and the napkin in their pockets, then roll the bundle and tie the ribbon to close it.

WHAT YOU NEED
per place setting

½ yard (.45 m) Irish linen for napkins

Measuring tape

Scissors

Sewing machine

Woven place mat

1 yard (.9 m) white grosgrain ribbon, 1½ inches (3.8 cm) wide

Straight pins

Knife, spoon, and fork

Fray retardant

DESIGNER: **ALLISON SMITH**

buffet place settings

customized food covers

DESIGNER: **KENNETH TRUMBAUER**

As soon as store aisles start filling with outdoor party supplies, you'll find wire-mesh food covers piled high. These inexpensive accessories are perfect for keeping food insect free, but the trouble is, they're drab. Here are two super-quick ways to perk them up and turn them into essential pieces of table decor.

WHAT YOU NEED

Domed food covers made of wire mesh
Clothing patches in bright floral or other summer designs
Beads in various sizes and coordinating colors
Hot-glue gun and glue sticks
Tape
Beading wire, 1¾ inch (4.4 cm)
Needle-nose pliers

BEADED COVER

1 Tape the beads to the dome where you want them. As with the patches, start with the larger beads first, then work your way down to the small ones. Rearrange as you go, if necessary.

2 Individually wire each bed to the dome. Thread a short length of wire through the bead, then through the dome's mesh. With the needle-nose pliers, push the wire back up through the mesh, and wrap it around the base of the bead to secure it tightly.

Don't cover your dome too heavily with patches or beads. You want the food underneath to be visible.

WHAT YOU DO

FLORAL PATCH COVER

1 Tape the patches to the dome where you want them, starting with large patches, then filling in with medium patches, and finally, small ones. Rearrange the patches until you're happy with the design.

2 One at a time, remove the tape from each patch, and glue it in place.

summer style

Freezer treats

I T'S SWELTERING, and your party isn't on the ice-cream truck route. No worry. Try these simple suggestions for frozen confections.

FRUIT ICE CUBES

Blend summer fruit and water, pour the mixture into an empty ice tray, and freeze. Pop the cubes into chilled glasses of ginger ale—or right into your mouth.

MAGIC ICE CREAM

Fill a small, freezer-safe, resealable bag halfway with milk. Add vanilla for flavor. Place the bag in another freezer-safe, resealable bag that's two or three times larger and packed with alternating layers of ice and rock salt. Seal the bag and shake it for a few minutes, and you've got ice cream.

YOGURT POPS

Blend fresh fruit with your favorite yogurt. Intensify the color of your yogurt pop with a few drops of food coloring, if you like. Pour the mixture into freezer-safe confection molds, add a candy stick to each, and freeze overnight. These make great breakfast delicacies.

FROZEN FRUIT CUP

Add sliced mandarin oranges, grapes, strawberries, and orange juice concentrate to a large bowl of applesauce. (Chunky applesauce works best.) Pour the mixture into individual bowls or small plastic cups and freeze. Remove from the freezer 30 minutes before serving.

BANANA POPS

Peel and halve three to five bananas. Cut off the sharp ends of several wooden skewers, then insert one lengthwise into each banana half. Spread yogurt onto the bananas, roll them in a crunchy cereal or granola, and place them on a cookie sheet covered with wax paper. Freeze them for at least an hour. Eat them frozen, just like yogurt pops.

CHOCOLATE BANANA POPS

Prepare the bananas as described for Banana Pops, and place them on a cookie sheet covered with wax paper. Melt chocolate in a bowl. Drizzle the chocolate on the bananas, turning the fruit to coat all sides. Freeze them for at least an hour.

POOCH POPS

Don't forget about your best friend. Blend yogurt, mashed bananas, and fruit juice. Add doggie treats, peanut butter, or whatever makes your dog sit up and bark. Blend. Pour and freeze the mixture in plastic-coated paper cups or in an empty ice tray. Remove the treats from the cups and serve on dog-day afternoons.

Ahhh, the simplicity of summer, when that emblem of outdoor fun—a big metal tub full of ice-cold bottles—can double as mood lighting. Set some out to illuminate pathways, cast dramatic shadows on your landscaping, or simply light the way to the refreshments.

WHAT YOU NEED

Galvanized tubs and flower pots

Strings of battery-powered mini-lights (available at many large craft stores, shops that specialize in holiday decorations, and lighting stores)

Ice

Bottled drinks

WHAT YOU DO

1 Place the tubs where you want your lighting.

2 Fill each tub with an abundant amount of mini-lights.

3 Of course, you don't want the lights near water, so to light up a tub of drinks and ice, position a small tub inside a larger one; fill the small tub with mini-lights, then surround it with ice and bottles.

DESIGNER: **SKIP WADE**

galvanized garden lighting

summer style

painted rock
place markers

DESIGNER: **ALLISON SMITH**

*Summertime gatherings seldom have formal seating
plans that specify who goes where. Still, these
spirited, easy-to-make place markers are a fun way
to liven up a table—and as a bonus, they'll help hold
the tablecloth and napkins in place on a breezy day.*

WHAT YOU NEED

Acrylic paints in bright summery colors:
    kiwi, banana, pool blue, etc.
Small artist's brush
Small flat river stones
Clear acrylic sealer

WHAT YOU DO

1 Dip the wooden end of the paintbrush into one paint color, then
dab it onto the rocks to make polka dots.

2 Repeat the process with all the paint colors until one side of each
rock is covered with multi-colored dots. Let them dry.

3 Turn the rocks over. Paint a name on the front of each. Use the
process described in steps 1 and 2 to make polka dots around the
edges of the front side. Let the rocks dry.

4 Spray each rock with a coat of clear acrylic sealer.

DESIGNER: **CHRIS RANKIN**

night light bouquet

Glowsticks—those luminous wands of impossibly brilliant color—have captivated kids at amusement parks (not to mention adults rocking out at concerts) for years. Why not use them as an inventive way to light up the night in your own backyard?

WHAT YOU NEED

Commercial glowsticks*

Glass vase

Glass marbles

*The long, thin glowsticks used at amusement parks and fairs come with a clip on each end, so you can shape them into circles or string them together. The shorter, thicker glowsticks sold at camping supply stores don't have a mechanism for binding them together, but you can make holes in their end wrappings with a hole punch, then bind them together with string or wire.

WHAT YOU DO

1 Wait until just before your gathering to start snapping the glowsticks and activating their chemicals. They'll lose their glow over the course of a few hours, so you'll want them to be at their strongest just as people arrive.

2 Fashion them into a centerpiece in a glass vase, with glass marbles functioning as flower frog in the base. Or, put them on display any number of ways:

- Tie them around napkins as napkin rings.
- Link them together into a strand of multicolored lights, and string them around a deck rail.
- Join their ends together to form circles or hoops you can wrap around outdoor furniture, tree branches, or shrubbery.

3 Glowsticks will start to fade after about four hours. Once your gathering is over, put the glowsticks in the freezer. The low temperature will refresh the chemicals, so you can use them again at the next party.

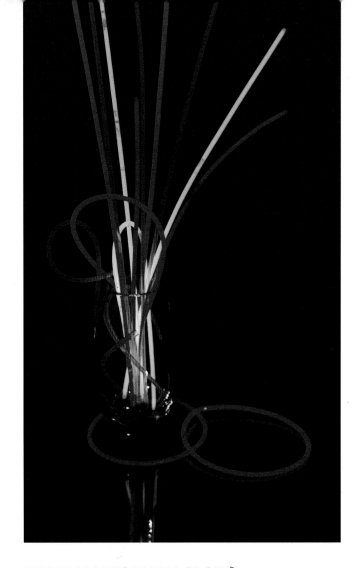

WHAT MAKES THEM GLOW?

Many chemical reactions produce both light and heat; think of a burning candle. Chemical reactions that produce light without heat create "cool light" or chemiluminescence. Fireflies are a natural example of this phenomenon. The glowstick is a man-made one.

HOW DO THEY WORK?

A thin glass ampule inside a glowstick breaks when it's bent. This results in the mixing and reaction of two chemicals that cause an "excited" state inside the glowstick. The chemicals "relax" to their normal state by dumping their energy into a fluorescent dye molecule in the stick. The dye releases the energy as brilliantly colored light.

colored block candlesticks

DESIGNER: **DIANA LIGHT**

When you want to be sure your guests understand that formal elegance is on summer break, you need some fanciful, sherbet-colored candleholders like these. Their building-block bodies swivel around, so you can even shift the color combinations mid-meal, if you like.

WHAT YOU NEED

8 2-inch (5.1 cm) wood blocks

Pencil

Ruler

Power drill

Wood-boring bits, ⅜ inch (9.5 mm), ²³⁄₆₄ inch (.9 cm), and ⅞ inch (2.2 cm)

Acrylic paints in red, orange, and yellow

Flat artist's brush, ½ inch (1.3 cm)

Palette

Rinse cup

Paper towels

Matte spray topcoat (optional)

2 ⁵⁄₁₆-inch (8 mm) wood dowels, at least 6 inches (15.2 cm) long

Big scissors to cut dowels to size

Craft glue or wood glue (optional)

2 ⅞-inch (2.2 cm) metal candle cup inserts

WHAT YOU DO

1 Find the center of each block and mark it lightly with a pencil on the top and bottom of each.

2 With the ²³⁄₆₄-inch (.9 cm) bit, drill about ¾ inch (1.9 cm) deep in the center of the tops of four blocks. Two of these blocks will be your base blocks (with the holes on their tops) and two will be your top blocks (with the holes on their bottoms).

3 On the other four blocks (the middle blocks), measure a point halfway between the center and a corner, and mark the spot on the tops and bottoms of the blocks. Be sure you mark the same corner on the top and bottom.

4 With the ⅜-inch (9.5 mm) bit, drill straight through each block, matching up the points you marked in step 3. To do so, drill halfway through from one hole, then drill the rest of the way from the other hole, so you get clean holes, with no splintering.

5 Wipe any dust off the blocks. Water down the acrylics on the palette, and paint the blocks, alternating the three colors on the top, sides, and bottom of each block. It's better to water the paints down too much rather than not enough. You can always paint over the blocks again if you need more color, but you're after a light, luminous look. Once you have the color saturation you want, let the blocks dry.

6 For added durability, you can spray the blocks with a matte topcoat. Let it dry.

7 Set the dowels in the bottom blocks, then thread the middle blocks onto the dowels. Position the top blocks on the dowels, and measure the distance between the top blocks and the blocks immediately below them. Take the top blocks off, pull the dowels out, and, with the big scissors, cut the amount you measured off the end of each dowel. Insert the rough, cut end of the dowels into the bottom blocks. Add a little wood or craft glue in the holes first, if you want extra stability.

8 With the ⅞-inch (2.2 cm) bit, drill out the center of the tops of the top blocks. Drill deeply enough so that the candle cup inserts will sit flush with the tops of the blocks.

9 Thread the middle blocks in place, and add the top blocks and the candle cup inserts.

Beyond briquettes

THOSE UNIFORM LITTLE CHARCOAL CUBES are as symbolic of summer as sandcastles and rubber flip-flops. But there may be times you want to infuse your smoked or grilled fare with a little added flavor. Here are some options.

HARDWOOD

You can replace briquettes completely by using this original grilling fuel in the form of logs, or you can add wood chunks or chips to a charcoal fire. Orchards are a good source for local woods. Others are available by mail order and at well-stocked stores that sell grilling tools and supplies. If you're using chunks or chips, soak them in water first, so they'll burn slowly and release their flavors more evenly in a mixture of smoke and water vapor.

WHITE OAK is typically thought of as a fuel for fireplaces and wood stoves, but it lends a nice flavor to grilled foods, especially chicken. Its mildly spiced smoke makes it a good wood to mix with others.

RED OAK works particularly well with pork and beef, and some say the dark-red wood darkens the color of whatever it cooks.

PECAN WOOD gives food a robust smoked flavor. It's ideal for hearty, dark meats.

HICKORY is probably the most famous smoking wood. It'll give everything from ribs to pork shoulder a good, strong flavor.

ALDER gives off a light flavor that works well with fish and poultry. In the northwestern United States, it's the traditional wood for smoking salmon.

MAPLE is another wood with a mellow smoke that provides a somewhat sweet flavor to poultry, pork, and seafood.

FRUITWOOD

Wood from apple, cherry, pear, and other fruit trees gives food a slightly sweeter taste than the savory smoke of hardwoods.

OTHER FUEL FOR FLAVORING

VINES such as grapevines make a tart, intensely flavored smoke. A little goes a long way, and vines aren't good for lengthy smoking.

HERBS, from oregano and rosemary to sage and thyme, will infuse meat with their particular flavorings. Use the wood stems of larger herb plants as well as the leaves. As with vines, you don't want to overdo it with herbs.

NUTSHELLS and **FRUIT PITS**, in most cases, can also add flavor to grilled and smoked foods. Try everything from coconut hulls (perfect for grilled fish) to peach pits.

FUEL TO AVOID

Evergreens; they contain heavy resins that will coat whatever you're cooking with a dark, bad-tasting film. Also, stay away from junk woods mixed with brush and scrap or treated lumber. Treated lumber likely contains toxic wood-preserving chemicals you don't want seeping into your food.

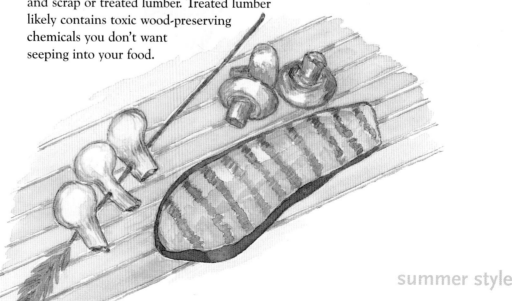

5
SUMMER STYLE

Lounging in the shade

Cultivated leisure is the aim of man.

—Oscar Wilde

Summer showers, lawn sprinklers, and the morning dew can all dampen your plans to spread out on that perfect spot under your favorite tree. Here's a way to convert any picnic blanket into one that keeps you nice and dry, despite slightly soggy ground underneath.

waterproof picnic blanket

DESIGNER: **LYNETTE COLBURN**

WHAT YOU NEED

Blanket or tablecloth

Ripstop nylon or another water-resistant fabric (You need a piece that's slightly bigger than your blanket or cloth.)

Scissors

Twill tape, 2 inches (5.1 cm) wide

Sewing machine

Fabric marker

Measuring tape or ruler

Hammer

Snap kit and snaps

WHAT YOU DO

1 Cut the nylon so it's ½ inch (1.3 cm) wider than your cloth or blanket on all sides.

2 Fold the edges of the nylon under ½ inch (1.3 cm), place twill tape on top of the edges, and machine stitch the inside and outside edges of the tape around the entire perimeter of the nylon.

3 Make marks for your snaps on the sewn twill tape, starting with each corner, then making a mark every 10 or 15 inches (25.4 or 38.1 cm), around the entire border of the blanket.

4 Following the instructions packaged with your snap kit, use the hammer to fix the snaps where you made marks. First, attach the "male" halves of the snaps to the backing. Then flip your blanket over, make matching marks for the "female" halves, and attach them.

5 Snap the backing to your cloth or blanket.

Section off a sizzling hot spot on your deck, and transform it into a shady retreat that draws people in. Here's a flexible design you can tailor to any setting.

deck awning

DESIGNER: **ALLISON SMITH**

WHAT YOU NEED

Standard measuring tools

Approximately 10 yards (9 m) of fabric (If you want to leave your awning up all the time, choose a fabric with a weatherproof coating. Otherwise, any mid to heavy-weight fabric is fine.)

Straight pins

Sewing machine

Iron

Grommet kit and ⅝-inch (1.6 cm) grommets

6 2½-inch (6.4 cm) flat aluminum C-brackets

4 large metal hooks

Drill and drill bit the size of your large metal hooks

3 8-foot (324.8 cm) wooden poles with removable finials

WHAT YOU DO

1 Measure the area you want your awning to cover. Add 16 inches (40.6 cm) to the length and 20 inches (50.8 cm) to the width.

2 Make note of the width of your fabric, and divide the calculated width dimension from step 1 by the fabric width to find out how many fabric panels you'll need to cut. Cut the fabric panels to the calculated length from step 1. Snipping the edge of the fabric and tearing it to length saves a lot of time.

3 Sew the panels together with French seams using the following process. Sew the first two together lengthwise, wrong sides facing, to make one large panel. Trim the allowances and press them open. Fold the fabric at the seam, rights sides facing (the raw edge will be hidden), and press again. Sew along the inside edge with a ⅝-inch [1.6 cm]) seam allowance. Unfold the fabric and press again on the seam. Repeat the process to add additional panels.

4 Subtract the width of the finished large panel you created in step 3 from the calculated width dimension from step 1. Divide the sum in half, and trim the amount from each side of the outside edges of the large fabric panel, if necessary. Before you cut away excess, make sure that the remaining fabric width equals the calculated width dimension.

5 Fold the outside edges under 1 inch (2.5 cm), and press them. Fold the edges under again 4½ inches (11.4 cm), and press a second time. Sew along the inside fold on both edges.

6 Finish the front edge of the awning by folding it under 1 inch (2.5 cm) and pressing it. Fold it under again 4½ inches (11.4 cm), and press a second time. Sew along the inside fold. Attach three grommets to this edge at the inside of the overhang. (Keep in mind that there's a 4½-inch [11.4 cm] overhang on the front and both sides. You need to place the grommets 4½ inches [11.4 cm] in from all edges.) Divide the width of the awning in half to find the center point, and center one grommet. Position the other two at equal distances from the center grommet.

7 Finish the awning along the house edge using the same process. Fold the edge in 2 inches (5.1 cm), and press. Fold it under again 2-1/2 inches (11.4 cm), and press a second time. Sew along the inside fold. Attach four grommets to this edge at the inside of the overhang on each side. Attach them to the folded reinforced fabric at the end, centering the second and third grommets between the first two.

8 Attach three brackets to the deck railing, so they line up with the placement of the grommets on the front edge of the awning. Attach three more brackets to the deck supports, making sure they line up with the first brackets. These will hold the awning's poles in place.

9 Drill pilot holes, then attach the hooks to the eve of the house, so they match the placement of the grommets on the house edge of the awning.

10 To attach the awning, hook the house edge in place first. Next, slip the poles into the brackets. Attach the poles to the front edge of the awning by threading the screws on the finial ends of the poles through the grommets, then screwing the finials in place.

SOME MEMBERS OF THE ANIMAL KINGDOM live farther away than others from oscillating fans. Here are a few ways those in the wild weather the heat.

Big cats, such as jaguars, are water-loving animals that take regular dips in the river to cool down. Their dens are typically in shady caves, where they can escape the summer sun.

Elephants find a luxurious mud bath the essence of summer relaxation. They use their trunks to coat their thick skin with mud that blocks out the heat and insects.

The hollow hairs of a polar bear's coat act as insulators, trapping cool air against their bodies. Their white coats also deflect sunlight, so their bodies don't absorb external heat.

A camel's hump stores fat, allowing the camel to live off what's in the hump when food is sparse during the driest desert seasons. The handy setup also prevents fat from spreading all over a camel's body and warming it up.

Kangaroo rats, who live in the desert, don't drink any water. Instead, they produce their own metabolically from the consumption of dry seeds. They also hole up in cool dens or burrows during the daytime to block out the heat and recycle the moisture from their own breathing.

Sand viper snakes use their saw-like dorsal scales to bury themselves in sand during the daytime. This acts as both a cooling strategy and an effective way to surprise prey.

Lions escape the dry African heat by sleeping up to 20 hours a day.

The round-tailed ground squirrel, which lives in the desert, sleeps through the hottest days of the summer, then hibernates in the winter.

Bat wings, elephant and rabbit ears, flamingo legs, goat horns, and human skin all radiate heat to provide cooling by evaporation.

How animals keep their cool

shades of blue lanterns

DESIGNER: **DIANA LIGHT**

WHAT YOU NEED

Tissue paper in shades of blue (or any color you like)

Ruler

Pen

Scissors

Iron

Pouch-style laminator (many copy shops have self-service machines)

Laminator pouch, 11 x 17 inches (27.9 x 43.2 cm)

3 no-sew snap fasteners per lantern

Craft knife

Hammer

Eyelet kit (These inexpensive kits contain eyelets and tools for attaching them; you'll need two small metal eyelets per lantern.)

Rag

1 thin aluminum coiling rod per lantern

Small wire cutters

Template for metal candle basket, page 126

.025-gauge aluminum sheet metal

Tape

Pencil

Work gloves

Straight tin snips

Small pliers

1 small, straight-sided glass votive holder and votive per lantern

By day, these luminaries can dangle on your porch or deck, their ultra-cool colors conjuring up thoughts of swimming pools and tropical bays. At night, light the votive candles inside, and they'll bathe everything in pastel light.

WHAT YOU DO

1 Cut the tissue paper so it measures 14½ x 10 inches (36.8 x 25.4 cm).

2 Use a warm iron to press the paper flat.

3 Laminate the paper, then trim the excess laminate, so you have a ⅛-inch (3 mm) border on three sides and a ¾-inch (1.9 cm) border on one of the short sides.

4 Set down three snaps on the short sides of the laminate. Position your snaps so the wider edge of laminate laps underneath the other. Before setting the snaps, mark where you want them by pressing the snap prongs into the laminate. Make sure they're ½ inch (1.3 cm) in from the edge. With the craft knife, cut small slits through where the prongs will go, then set the snaps according the instructions on the snap packaging.

5 To identify points for attaching the lantern handle, measure in 4 inches (10.2 cm) from each short side. Mark those points about ½ inch (1.3 cm) down from the top of the laminate, and carefully cut a small X at each point with the craft knife.

6 Set a metal eyelet at each point, following the packaging instructions. You'll use the hammer and the tool packaged with the eyelets. It's a good idea to place a rag underneath the points when you hammer to protect both your work surface and the eyelet.

7 With wire cutters, cut the coiling rod into a 12-inch (30.5 cm) piece. Use small pliers to bend up both ends about ¼ inch (6 mm) from the ends. Attach the upturned ends through the metal eyelets.

8 Size the template for the candle basket on a photocopy machine, cut it out, and tape it to the aluminum sheet metal. Trace around it with the pencil.

9 Wearing gloves, carefully cut out the piece with tin snips, and bend up each arm of the piece to create a basket.

10 Snap the laminated sheet into a cylinder. Use small pliers to bend the ends of the longer basket arms, so they'll hook over the laminated cylinder.

11 Place a votive in the basket, and lower it into the cylinder.

Painting on glass has become one of the hottest decorating trends going, probably because the paints are so easy to apply, and they produce such terrific results. Here's how to use them to turn a plain pitcher and glasses into a colorful set to cool off with.

DESIGNER: **DIANA LIGHT**

painted lemonade pitcher & glasses

summer style

WHAT YOU NEED

Pitcher and glasses

Plain paper

Templates for circles in various sizes
    (Jar lids work well.)

Pen or pencil

Scissors

Tape

Air-dry, opaque glass paints in two shades
    of yellow and two shades of blue

Surface conditioner, if your paints call for it

Round artist's brush, about ¼ inch (6 mm)

Flat artist's brush, about ½ inch (1.3 cm)

Towels for nestling glasses as you paint

Rinse water

Cotton swabs

WHAT YOU DO

1 Clean and dry the glass.

2 Trace circles onto the paper, cut them out, arrange them randomly on the insides of the glass pieces, and tape them in place.

3 If you're using surface conditioner, brush it on the glass with the flat brush, and let it dry. Reapply it if necessary, following the conditioner's packaging instructions.

4 Working on the outside of the glass and using the round brush, paint some of the larger circles with one shade of yellow and the rest with the other shade of yellow. Use a wet cotton swab to clean up small mistakes as you work. Let the paint dry.

5 On each yellow circle, use the opposite yellow to lay down sunburst-like brush strokes that extend from the inside of the circle to the outside edges. Let the paint dry.

6 Paint the smaller circles with one shade of blue. With the other blue, paint connecting lines among the circles, some straight and some squiggly. Let the paints dry, according to their packaging instructions. Remove the paper templates.

IF IT'S AN ESPECIALLY LONG, SULTRY SUMMER, you're going to need an easy new thirst quencher to rotate with the iced tea and fresh-squeezed lemonade. Here it is.

A few handfuls of fresh,
   clean mint leaves
Can of pineapple juice
Ice

1 Mix the mint and pineapple juice in a blender until it's finely pureed. Pour it into a large pitcher and chill.

2 To serve, blend the pineapple-mint puree with ice in a blender until the ice is crushed and the beverage is frothy. Add a mint leaf to each for a garnish, and serve immediately.

Pineapple mint coolers

If you plan to dress up quite a few drinks this summer, spring for a channel knife. Its V-shaped blade does a better job than a vegetable peeler of cleanly cutting fruit rind for twists.

Save the Spanish olives and those smart little cocktail onions for some quiet evening in February. Summer is a time when we want our liquid refreshments to look as festive as we feel, sporting twists, twirls, wedges, spears, and cherries on top. Here are a few easy favorites.

ORANGE SPIRAL

Use a channel knife or vegetable peeler to cut a narrow strip of orange peel. Press firmly and keep the pressure even as you cut, so you don't end up with a strip that's too thin. Hook one end of the strip on the glass, and twirl the rest around the stem.

LEMON ZEST

Cut a strip of lemon peel, following the same tips described for cutting the orange spiral. Twine it around inside the glass. Make a small cut in the middle of a lemon round, so you can slip it onto a straw. Add the embellished straw to the glass.

STRAWBERRY SLICES

Slice one large and one small strawberry in half. Spear the back of the large strawberry half with a toothpick. Using a little lemon juice, stick the sliced side of the small strawberry to the sliced side of the large one. With the help of the toothpick, balance the pair on the edge of the glass, and add a mint leaf as backdrop.

PINEAPPLE STALKS

Cut two squared-off strips of pineapple. Make sure they're tall enough to stand up in the glass, with one about ½ inch (1.3 cm) longer than the other. Stand the stalks in place, and use a toothpick to top the tallest with a cherry.

DESIGNER: **SKIP WADE**

drink garnishes

bubble wands

DESIGNER: **ALLISON SMITH**

These whimsical wands are so easy to twist together, you can assemble an entire bouquet in no time. Use them to lift bubbles into the summer sky, or gather them in a bunch for a spritied display of garden art.

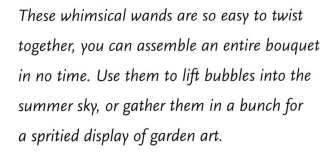

WHAT YOU NEED

½-inch (1.3 cm) dowel rod, 12 inches (30.5 cm) long
Fine sandpaper
Drill with small drill bit
3 feet (91.5 cm) of thin copper wire
Needle-nose pliers with wire cutters
Button (optional)
Hot glue gun and glue stick (optional)

WHAT YOU DO

1 Sand off the ends of the dowel rod.

2 Drill a hole 1 inch (2.5 cm) down from one end of the rod.

3 Thread one end of your wire through the hole, leaving approximately 6 inches (15.2 cm) of wire as a tail.

4 Coil the tail around the dowel rod.

5 With the pliers, twist the rest of the wire into a heart, star, or flower shape. Make sure you complete the shape at the top of the dowel rod.

6 Twist the two ends of wire together, and coil it decoratively at the front of the bubble wand. Snip off any excess, if necessary.

7 For the "flower," attach a large button to the center of the flower with a dab of hot glue.

hammocks 101

DESIGNER: **CHRIS RANKIN**

If there's a universal symbol of summertime repose, the hammock is it. Position one under your favorite tree, and it's the visual cue that you've made the switch to summer hours. Here's a primer with the basics of buying and hanging a hammock, along with some tidbits of hammock history you can toss out as you lounge.

HANGING HOW-TO

Before you begin, do a little backyard reconnaissance. You need two trees to anchor your hammock. Once you identify the ones you think will work, lie beneath them and imagine yourself suspended about four feet (120 cm) up. Do you like what you see? Then go ahead and hang your hammock there.

WHAT YOU NEED

A friend

A hammock

2 hook screws or 2 screw eyes (use the screw eyes if your hammock didn't come with a metal ring at each end) and 2 S-hooks

Electric drill and a bit slightly smaller than the width of the hook screws or screw eyes

Vice grips or screwdriver

WHAT YOU DO

1 After you've picked the perfect spot for your hammock, give your friend one end while you grab the other, and figure out how high you want your hammock to hang. Remember that your hammock will sink down when you get in it. To adjust its height upward, either move the spot where you'll put the hooks higher up the tree trunks, or find a spot that lets you position the hooks farther apart. Mark the places for your hooks in each tree trunk.

2 Drill a hole in the trunk of each tree.

3 Screw in the hook screws or screw eyes. Use the vice grip to tighten the hook screws or a screwdriver to tighten the screw eyes.

4 Hang your hammock on the hook screws. If you've used screw eyes, add the S-hooks as connectors.

If your backyard is lacking in proper hammock-hanging trees, consider buying a free-standing hammock or planting posts in your yard. We recommend pouring a bit of concrete into your postholes to make sure the posts remain stable.

BUYING BASICS

■ If you want your hammock to hang out in all sorts of weather, get one made with synthetic rope, which will resist rot. But when comfort is your key consideration, nothing beats an all-cotton hammock—just be sure to bring it inside during inclement weather.

■ Will you be snuggling up with someone in your hammock? Better get a double (sometimes called a matrimonial). If you're not about to share your special space, a single hammock will do.

■ The only other major consideration in hammock-buying is this: do you want a hammock with spreader bars, or do you want a Mayan-style hammock that wraps around you like a cocoon? There are advantages to both; give each style a test ride to see which one suits you best. With spreader-bar hammocks, the more ropes coming through the bars the better.

HAMMOCK HISTORY

Leave it to an advanced culture to treat relaxation as a fine art. Historians of the hammock credit the ancient Mayans with developing the first web-like recliner approximately 1,000 years ago. Those who have studied and adapted the design say it's one of the most ingenious and comfortable ever. Later, natives of South and Central America let their sturdy fishing nets do double duty as hanging beds. The trend migrated as sailors arriving in the New World adopted the custom. Among the Wapisiana Indians of Guyana, a hammock was the traditional gift a woman gave to her groom on their wedding day. Now, people around the world consider hammocks central to a happy marriage.

I**F YOU HAVE A HARD TIME INDULGING** in a lazy, summer-afternoon nap, try reading a few statistics to lull yourself into dreamland. Like the one about how tens of millions of us are chronically sleep deprived. Or maybe the one about how people who get enough sleep are better at everything from playing the piano to driving a car. Then lie back, settle in, and treat yourself to some shut-eye.

In many countries, businesses close from 1 p.m. to 4 p.m. to give employees—and anyone who might otherwise be tempted to shop—a siesta. In Spain, Portugal, and Italy, establishments rent resting spots to traveling nappers. Geniuses like Leonardo da Vinci and Albert Einstein swore by napping for rejuvenation. And Sir Winston Churchill went so far as to change into his Pj's for his regular naps.

Fortunately for nap neophytes, summer provides the perfect setting for practice: long afternoons, with temperatures too high to do much of anything else. Experts say you need only 20 or 30 minutes to feel revived. In fact, you really don't even have to drift off. Just kicking back, closing your eyes, and resting your bones a while leaves you refreshed and ready for when the shops open again.

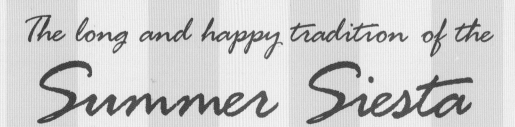

The long and happy tradition of the
Summer Siesta

Sure, you can buy standard-issue drink umbrellas at any party-supply store. But when it's this easy to make your own elegant, customized assortment, why not shade your summer drinks in ultimate style?

cocktail parasols

DESIGNER: **DIANA LIGHT**

WHAT YOU NEED

Soup can, mug, or other circular shape
    to use as a guide

Piece of scrap paper

Pencil

Scissors

Decorative paper stiff enough to hold its shape
    (Origami paper works especially well.)

Decorative-edge scissors

Craft glue

Toothpick

Bamboo skewers

Small beads
    (optional)

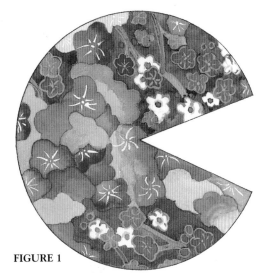

FIGURE 1

WHAT YOU DO

1 Trace around your circular object, transferring a circle to the scrap of paper. Cut out the circle.

3 Fold the circle in half, then in quarters, then in eighths, then unfold the paper. Where the folds cross in the center of the circle, use the pencil to poke a small hole in the center.

4 Cut out one of the eight pie sections.

5 Use your template to trace as many circles as you need on the decorative paper, tracing on the back side of the paper. Cut them out with regular or decorative-edge scissors.

6 Center the plain-paper stencil on the decorative-paper circles, mark the cut-out piece, and cut the piece out of each circle (see figure 1).

7 Bring the straight edges together, overlapping them slightly, to form each circle into a cone shape. Using the end of the toothpick, spread a small bit of glue on the straight edges and attach them. If you want some of your parasols to have accordion-like pleats, make them before you glue them into cones. Start at one straight edge, and fold the paper over, under; over, under; and so on, folding around the whole circle.

8 Put a small bit of glue on the inside tips of the cones, and push the pointed ends of skewers through the tips, so about ⅛ inch (3 mm) of the skewer ends are showing.

9 If you like, add bead embellishments to the ends of the skewers.

10 Snip the other ends of the skewers to adjust the heights of the parasols, if necessary.

122

These cheerful fans are so enchanting, just looking at them will make you swear you feel a breeze. Gather a bunch in a colorful bucket; stand them upright in pails of sand (or wedges of watermelon); or hand them out, wait one second, and watch wrists start gently waving.

paper fans

DESIGNER: **ALLISON SMITH**

WHAT YOU NEED

Scrapbook papers in
    complementary colors

Ruler

Pencil

Scissors

Large craft sticks

Colored craft wire

Craft glue

Clothespins

WHAT YOU DO

1 Stack the paper and measure its width. Divide the width by two. Subtract 1 inch (2.5 cm) from the width, and make a note of the number, then add 1 inch (2.5 cm) to the width, and make a note of that number. Cut the paper into two pieces using the two measurements. (For example, if the paper is 10 inches [25.4 cm] wide, half the width is 5 inches [12.7 cm]. Subtract 1 inch [2.5 cm], and you get 4 inches [10.2 cm]. Add 1 inch [2.5 cm], and get 6 inches [15.2 cm]). The goal is to end up with two strips of paper, one slightly smaller than the other.

2 Stack two different paper colors, one piece smaller and one larger, with the smaller piece centered on top of the larger. Fold them accordion style, with the depth of the folds matching the width of the craft sticks.

3 Holding the folded accordion in one long strip, trim the ends at a 45° angle. Tightly secure the center of the accordion with a small piece of colored wire. When you finish, the wired piece should look like a bow tie.

4 Pull up the two top edges of the bow tie, and glue the edges together, holding them with clothespins until the glue dries.

5 Attach a craft stick to each bottom edge of the bow tie with glue. Hold everything in place with clothespins until the glue dries.

6 Remove the clothespins, join the craft sticks, and wrap a small piece of wire around the sticks to keep the fan open.

Ice cream:
Summer's fifth food group

NEXT TIME YOU START TO STOP YOURSELF from ordering that triple scoop of quadruple chocolate in a waffle cone, consider this. Human tongues are programmed to crave sweet, fatty foods. All of the carbohydrates our early ancestors ate as their main source of energy were sweet. For them, eating sweet foods was never confused with hedonistic pleasure; it was purely a matter of survival. What better way to ensure your own survival on a wiltingly hot summer afternoon than by indulging in a sundae, a shake, or a cone topped with a scoop or two of your favorite flavor?

The origins of ice cream are a bit murky. Some say it was first served in ancient Rome. Others maintain that ice cream didn't exist until the 17th century. But we know that making ice cream at home became a widespread practice following American Nancy Johnson's invention of the hand-cranked ice cream maker in 1846. Today, thanks to all kinds of electric ice cream makers, churning up a customized batch of ice cream in your own kitchen is as easy as pie—easier! Start with a vanilla ice cream, and you can make any flavor you can dream up. Simply prep the ingredients, if necessary, and add them just before your ice cream freezes.

here's a starter list of possibilities:

BLACK FOREST ICE CREAM
sweet cherries and chocolate syrup

MANGO ICE CREAM
fresh mangoes

GINGER ICE CREAM
candied ginger pieces

MOCHA ICE CREAM
coffee and chocolate syrup

COOKIE DOUGH ICE CREAM
balls of cookie dough

GREEN TEA ICE CREAM
brewed green tea

PINEAPPLE ICE CREAM
fresh pineapple chunks

STRAWBERRY WHITE CHOCOLATE ICE CREAM
strawberries and white chocolate chips

PEANUT BUTTER ICE CREAM
chunky or smooth peanut butter

LEMONADE ICE CREAM
thawed lemonade concentrate

bonus scoop

In case you finally tire of the classic combination of cream and ice (just pretend), here's a quick primer for your next trip to a well-stocked frozen sweet shop.

SORBET or SORBETTO: This traditional European treat is a frozen mix of fruit juice, sugar, and water.

GRANITA: A variation on sorbet, granita has a grainier texture than its predecessor.

SHERBET: Coming to us courtesy of medieval Persia, sherbet is a flavored ice thickened with eggs whites and gelatin.

SIMPLE PAINTED SWING, PAGE 39

SHADES OF BLUE LANTERNS, PAGE 108

LAWN CHAIR REVIVAL, PAGE 44

contributors

LYNETTE COLBURN has been creating clothing, textiles, and paintings for years. This marks her design debut with Lark Books.

DIANA LIGHT lives and works in the beautiful Blue Ridge Mountains of North Carolina. Her home studio, like her life, is surrounded by glittering glass in hundreds of forms, styles, and types. After earning her BFA in painting and printmaking, she extended her expertise to etching and painting fine glass objects. She has contributed to numerous Lark books and is the coauthor of Lark's *The Weekend Crafter: Etching Glass*.

TRACY MUNN is a sewing dynamo. When she's not making a slipcover for anything not nailed down, she's doing upholstery in her studio in a converted barn. She also teaches home decor classes at a local college, but her favorite sewing activity is designing dresses for her two granddaughters, Chaley and Chloe. She's the author of the new Lark book, *Simple Slipcovers*.

ROB PULLEYN is president of Lark Books, and is usually a very hands-off manager. But when the spirit moves him, he can't help using his hands to create projects for our books. He lives in the mountains of western North Carolina.

CHRIS RANKIN is a multi-talented designer and the author of several Lark books, including *Splendid Samplers* and *Creative Lighting for Outdoor Living*.

ALLISON SMITH lives in Asheville, North Carolina. Her home-based business specializes in providing deluxe tourist accommodations in remote locations around the world. She's an avid crafter and designer in addition to being a full-time mother. She has created projects for numerous Lark books, including *Decorating Baskets*, *Girls' World*, and *Decorating Candles*.

TERRY TAYLOR lives and works in Asheville, North Carolina, as an editor and project coordinator for Lark Books. He is a prolific designer and exhibiting artist, and works in media ranging from metals and jewelry to paper crafts and mosaics. Some of the most recent Lark books to which he has contributed include *Creative Outdoor Lighting*, *Salvage Style*, and *The Book of Wizard Craft*.

KENNETH TRUMBAUER has worked in the field of visual merchandising since the mid-1980s. In addition to handling freelance projects for numerous clients, he has worked with retailers such as Saks Fifth Avenue, Pier 1 Imports, Neiman Marcus, and Biltmore Estate in Asheville, North Carolina. He most recently contributed to Lark's *Simple Flower Style*.

SKIP WADE makes a living making people and places look good. Specializing in fashion and domestics, he works in both still photography and film as a photo stylist, prop master, wardrobe manager, and location scout. He and his partner live in Asheville, North Carolina, where they're continually renovating a 1920s house. He has contributed his talents to several Lark books, including *The New Book of Table Settings*, *Decorating Porches and Decks*, and *Decorating with Mini-Lights*.

JANE WILSON spent many years as a studio designer, after studying art history and design at East Tennessee University and technical drawing and drafting at Eastern Kentucky University. She has designed for various Lark books, including *The Complete Book of Garden Seating*.

index

A NOTE ABOUT SUPPLIERS

Usually, the supplies you need for making the projects in Lark books can be found at your local craft supply store, discount mart, home improvement center, or retail shop relevant to the topic of the book. Occasionally, however, you may need to buy materials or tools from specialty suppliers. In order to provide you with the most up-to-date information, we have created a list of suppliers on our Web site, which we update on a regular basis. Visit us at www.larkbooks.com, click on "Craft Supply Sources," and then click on the relevant topic. You will find numerous companies listed with their web address and/or mailing address and phone number.